Tales of Old Herefordshire

Other counties in this series include:

Avon
Berkshire
Buckinghamshire
Cambridgeshire
East Anglia
Essex
Gloucestershire
Hampshire
Hertfordshire
Kent
Lincolnshire

Northamptonshire
Oxfordshire
Somerset
Stratford
Suffolk
Surrey
Sussex
Warwickshire
Wiltshire
Worcestershire

Tales of Old Herefordshire

Kathleen Lawrence-Smith

With Illustrations by Don Osmond

COUNTRYSIDE BOOKS
NEWBURY, BERKSHIRE

ISBN 1 85306 088 7

Produced through MRM Associates Ltd., Reading
Typeset by Acorn Bookwork, Salisbury
Printed in England by J. W. Arrowsmith Ltd., Bristol

To my husband, Ray, whose keen
interest in this work has reconciled
him to many lonely days

Acknowledgements

I am grateful to the following for their assistance, encouragement and permission to quote from works of which they hold copyright or other rights of recognition:

The Woolhope Naturalists' Field Club for material on fungus forays

The Bulmer family and Hereford Cider Museum Trust regarding early days of cider production.

Phillimore & Co. Ltd., publishers of *The Leon Valley* by norman Reeves, for the tale of the drunken ducks.

Chatto & Windus, publishers of Margaret Forster's graphic portrayal in *Elizabeth Barrett Browning, A Biography*.

Mrs Veronica Harland, daughter of the late W.H. Howse, author of *The History and Legend of Stapleton Castle*.

The Estate of H.L.V. Fletcher for a quotation from *Portrait of the Wye Valley* published by Robert Hale Ltd.

Col. T.J.B. Hill, M.B.E., and *The Hereford Times* for material on Lt. Col. Fitzwilliam Chipp's career.

The Rector and villagers of Edvin Ralph for their details of the village legend.

To Hugh Lasgarn, Herefordshire Vet and author, for friendly encouragement and advice on sources.

Contents

HEREFORDSHIRE: The map overleaf is by John Speede and shows the county as it was in the early seventeenth century.

Gold
in the
Orchard

THE strong bond of family affection at Credenhill rectory in the 1830s provided the springboard for one of Herefordshire's most outstanding enterprises. There was less than two years between the rector's two sons, but the devotion which existed between them might well have stirred the envy of parents everywhere from Adam and Eve onwards. Yet they were quite different in temperament. Fred had an outgoing personality with a lively sense of humour, was somewhat impulsive and ready to defend with vigour a cause or principle which excited him. Percy was quieter, more reserved in manner, almost shy yet with a ready will to show kindness and consideration when needed.

Unfortunately (or so it seemed at the time) Percy, the younger son, suffered ill health in childhood and missed the chance of a formal education and of following his brother to boarding school and university. Inevitably their interests and attainments diverged. While Fred was still enjoying his time at King's College, Cambridge, reading Classics and finding great delight in the world of good literature, Percy, at 20 and now with greatly improved health, was faced with an uncertain future. How to make a living in a competitive world without qualifications to point in any specific direction? 'If you're going into business,' advised his mother with the sound commonsense which had endeared her to the parish, 'do something connected with eating or drinking. They do not go out of fashion!' That advice and the rectory orchards provided the answer. Percy found the pot of gold in his own backyard – or his father's, which proved to be even better, for the rector had become something of an authority on orcharding, apple and pear production, perry and cider. Percy Bulmer squared up to the challenge in 1887 – the year of Queen Victoria's Jubilee.

With the loan of a neighbour's old-fashioned stone mill and the docile co-operation of the family pony *Tommy*, the Glebe Orchard provided the first rung of the cidermaker's ladder. Brother Fred, during the Long Vacation from Cambridge, lent a willing hand and within a year a promising beginning brought a move to the city of Hereford five miles away. Percy's father put his money into his faith in his son. He purchased an acre of land in Ryelands Street for £350 and, at some sacrifice, raised £1,760 to build and equip a one-storey shack with cellar below. Brother Fred came again to give a hand and set the wheels in motion before returning to Cambridge. But it is unlikely that any one of them, in his wildest dreams, imagined that this was the cider factory which was to become the biggest producer in the world!

When the rector and his wife had arrived in Herefordshire, it was obvious that hundreds of the county's 30,000 acres of orcharding were suffering from decay and neglect, and that the Credenhill area was ripe for a revival of production. The county's asset had been neglected or, at least, underestimated. The rector contributed on the subject to the press, the *Journal of Horticulture* and to Volume 1 of *The Herefordshire Pomona*. Now, through his son, he was putting words into action. Perhaps the most amazing investment of all, however, came from Fred, who came down from university and abandoned his promising career in the scholastic world to sink his life, energies and talents into his younger brother's enterprise. Fred had earned a Second Class Honours Degree in Classics, a Half Blue for Athletics and gained a host of congenial friends at King's College, finally being offered the post of tutoring the sons of the King of Siam. He chose to let it all go to join the family business. Perhaps it was as well – 'Fred and the King of

Siam' would not have had half the appeal that the story of the famous Anna has done!

It was fortunate that Fred had no illusions about the task he had undertaken alongside his brother or he could never have stood the rigours of the working day that began before 6 am. A hasty bread and cheese lunch sufficed until the evening, when a messenger boy from Credenhill arrived at the railway station with a pewter pot of supper sent by their mother. It would be 10 pm before they sank to the shack floor and fell asleep – if they were lucky! Sometimes they were up all night, or maybe snatched only the odd couple of hours sleep before dawn. Then they would be wakened by an old cottager living nearby, christened Thomas but known more affectionately as 'Tummas' and taken on the staff. He brought them tea brewed on the cottage hob all night and – on red letter mornings – a plate of chopped, fried chitterlings. Probably few of the delicacies which came their way later achieved such succulence. Tummas was worthy of his hire, though how they met the wage bill is a puzzle seeing that on their 'early finishing day' (Saturdays at 6 pm) they walked the five miles home to save train fare. Fourpence each!

Remarkably Fred Bulmer kept the delightful friendships made at university. He confessed to the 'uncongenial labour' of his situation, but inspired in his friends such understanding that several of them made investments in the firm almost at the point of sacrifice. Inevitably the brothers had reverses, and their position was so delicate financially that several times they came near to toppling over the edge.

The family solicitor was an uncle by marriage and godfather to Fred. Not long after the firm became operative, he joined his nephews at their frugal lunch, seated himself on a cider case alongside, accepted their ill-afforded hospitality and genially enquired about their progress. They needed more space desperately – of necessity and not mere ambition, doubting if they could carry on otherwise. It so happened the remaining acres of the site on which they sat were up for sale. They needed just two acres alongside the one their father had purchased for them.

The godfather brushed the crumbs from his lap, smiled his

farewells, took himself off to the vendor and bought the ten acres on the market. In a few weeks Percy offered him £800 for two acres (he had paid just over £300 per acre) – and was met with a curt refusal! 'I have got you now and I mean to bleed you!' was the incredible retort. It was enough to destroy faith in human nature, let alone family ties – had not the most amazing coincidence occurred. The solicitor and the owner died on the same night! The contract for the sale of the site had to be quickly taken over by another purchaser. A second uncle-by-marriage stepped in, took it over and conveyed it to Fred and Percy on mortgage at the most benign terms imaginable. Two years later they sold off three acres, paid off the entire mortgage and owned all the land they wanted, free of actual cost. Small wonder Percy fell in love with that uncle's daughter and later married her!

For 30 years the brothers' idyllic partnership continued – exciting, exhausting, exasperating and exhilarating years as recorded by Fred Bulmer in his excellent little book *Early Days of Cider Making*. By trial and error each brother found his particular bent. Percy hastily abandoned a trial role as salesman; when a mother wrote in later years asking for a job for her son, he replied 'The only vacancy we have is for a commercial traveller. This, however, requires rare and special gifts and a man may well thank his God if he does not possess them.' Percy's own speciality lay in management of the growing firm and his elder brother has written of his great – almost uncanny – sense of judgement and decisive action. Fred took on the role of travelling salesman, more from necessity than choice. It could not have come naturally to a man with an academic background, but he recalls with glee in his book that Percy once acknowledged receipt of an order by telegraphing back 'WELL DONE THOU GOOD AND FAITHFUL TOUTER'. It was a relief all round when the right man came along to represent the firm and bring in the orders.

So the busy years went on, experimenting with flavours, developing sidelines such as pectin, Pecta Puree, non-alcoholic Cidona, and travelling around the Continent as news of new skills and alternative methods reached them. And as demands for the family cider increased, apples and pears had to be sought and purchased from other orchards, the quality examined and supplies assured to feed the Bulmer factory in times of plenty and of drought, at whatever price could be negotiated in prevailing circumstances.

Both brothers were fully stretched. But happily they somehow found time for romance, one on his own doorstep, so to speak, and the elder one on the Continent. So, in the course of time, a second and third generation emerged to follow on in the family tradition and make the labels *Woodpecker, Pomagne, Strongbow, Limelight, Ciderkin, Dry Cider* and *Draught Cider* household names, while H. P. Bulmer Limited became the biggest cider making enterprise in the world.

Towards the end of his life, Fred Bulmer (who was the successor of the two brothers) wrote with sympathy of business founders who have no family capable of maintaining their enterprise and adds 'No such dilemma has confronted me. All the boys have good hearts, good heads and good morals and I can leave the business to them with an easy conscience.' Experience has proved that his confidence was not misplaced and Herefordshire is grateful for it.

The Mystery
of the
Mappa Mundi

THE Mappa Mundi is the only map of its kind and anti-
quity which is known to have survived in its entirety. The
sheet of vellum, made from calfskin, is over five feet high and
four feet six inches wide and is closely covered with graphic
illustrations which portray the teeming life behind each carefully placed location. It is not merely a link up of routes and
place names; it is a pictorial history of the world as it was
known in the 13th century. It is an encyclopaedia contained in
a circle; the combination of text, drawings and painted scen-
ery produces a veritable work of art which is almost mind-
boggling at first sight.

It was the late 13th century when Richard of Haldingham
put the finishing touches to his Map of the World. He could
justifiably add his signature with a flourish, for this was the
culmination of 20 years of painstaking endeavour, of assi-
duous attention to detail. Experts find it hard to believe that a
churchman had sufficient free time, even in 20 years, to
accomplish so great a task. And this is only part of the mystery
which surrounds this priceless treasure of Hereford Cathedral.

One wonders how the artist could begin to formulate such a
great enterprise. He would, of course, have had the benefit of
older histories and his copy of the Scriptures, with their
wealth of illumination on the movements of man and his
doings over 5,000 turbulent years. And it seems likely that

contemporary touches, which Richard adds here and there, were the result of his listening to travellers' tales, returning Crusaders, pilgrims, soldiers and merchants from near and far. He must have been an avid reader and a good listener with a lively imagination. His ready grasp gives rise to the thought that in the heart of this cloistered cleric lurked a suppressed yearning for travel and adventure. Did he then find fulfilment in the great work which occupied his drawing board for those 20 years? Was this his window on the world?

Richard began his first tentative brush strokes by placing the Holy Land in the centre of his circle, with the walled city of Jerusalem and 'Mount Calvarie' as his focal point, then moving outwards to other Biblical locations. The Mediterranean, like other seas, was painted green while blue-painted rivers thread their way inland through the mass of towns and cities, blancmange-shaped mountain ranges, castellated towers and a pathetic little unclothed figure which must be Lot's wife looking sadly back on the scene of her undoing. Ancient monasteries are featured along the banks of the Nile as are strange beasts with near-human heads, mermaids and mermen, fire-snorting dragons and other strange apparitions recorded in mythology. Noah's Ark, perched on an Armenian mountain, is enlivened by the heads of serpents and birds peeping through portholes. Recognisable forms are those of the unicorn, the rhinoceros, the elephant, the lion, the leopard and the tiger, all carefully placed in the setting provided by travellers' tales.

Some very odd human creatures also emerge – people without ears, with tiny mouths which can take nourishment only through a tube, a keen-sighted race shown with four eyes each, people whose heads seem to be in their breasts and even dog-headed people.

The drawings and text (in Norman French) are in bold black ink and a number of intriguing little tales are neatly worked in between scenes. How else could we know that the Bonnacon, with its bull's head, horse's mane and curling horns, is capable, when chased, of discharging dung over three acres? And if the smell were not sufficient to discourage his pursuer, the acid content which burned where it touched must have given the Bonnacon the final word and unchallenged supremacy.

Even plant life is not without its wonders. Roots like feet, trunks like bodies surmounted by human-looking features and hair-like foliage, are there to astonish the eye and reveal the wonders hidden to most of us.

Europe is somewhat contorted into the outer rim of the flat circle. But it is clearly there, with towns famous in medieval times emerging between the Baltic, the Rhine, the Seine, the Danube, the Thames, the Severn and the Dee, with numerous islands dotted around the misty green seas. Undeterred by his difficulty in fitting Great Britain against this outer rim, Richard has divided it into the four sections of England, Cornwall, Wales and Scotland, with a rather elongated Ireland alongside.

It is regrettable that so little is known about the origins of this map. Hereford Cathedral authorities confess that their possession of it is part of the mystery surrounding it. They possess no title deeds or documentation about it. And we know tantalisingly little about the artist, which is disappointing because the public always wants to know something of the personality behind a great work. The artist's full signature appears in the bottom left hand corner as 'Richard of Haldingham and Lafford', now recognised to be Holdingham and Sleaford in Lincolnshire. So he must have had a long association with that county during the making of the map. Experts date the commencement of the work as around 1269 and it appears that Lincoln Cathedral, at that very time, provided unrivalled facilities to assist map-makers. Despite the hesitation of some researchers to commit themselves, it is tempting to agree with those who believe that the Richard de Bello who was a prebendary of Holdingham and Sleaford and thereby connected with Lincoln Cathedral during that period, was indeed the artist.

By 1289, when it is thought likely that the map was being completed, a Richard de Bello is found to be a Canon of Hereford Cathedral. This seems to provide the missing link and to show why Hereford and not Lincoln inherited this treasure. Did the artist bring his almost completed work with him to Hereford? It does appear that the location of Hereford on the map was rather sketchily etched in at a late stage. This serves to show on how slender a thread an inheritance may hang, and why Hereford confesses that its ownership of the Mappa Mundi is an unsolved mystery.

Nevertheless, if it is true that possession is nine points of the law, Hereford will not be challenged. Richard was content to leave his map where, when seen, a prayer might be raised for the good of his soul and for his welfare in the world beyond that of the Mappa Mundi. He left a note to this effect beneath his signature. What a splendid thing it would be if, there, he were deputed to make a map of the Heavens and the universe with its even greater mysteries!

The Barretts of Hope End

ON a chill November day in 1809, three year old Elizabeth Moulton Barrett skipped her way from the coach which had brought her with her family to their new home. Little Elizabeth was destined to go down in history for her part in a great love story, but long before her family were the Barretts of Wimpole Street, they were the Barretts of Hope End, a Georgian mansion four miles east of Ledbury.

It has been suggested that the house's obscurity is what appealed to 24 year old Edward Barrett. It was tucked away at the end of a winding labyrinth of paths, completely lost to view from the roadway. But once inside the grounds a new world opened up for the newcomers. The spacious property contained a deer park, a stream meandering through the grounds and masses of abundant foliage to encourage its plentiful birdlife.

Very soon after their arrival the father of the family earned for himself the teasing title which his eldest daughter later bestowed upon him – the Monarch of Hope End. Quite oblivious to anyone else's opinion or advice he began to build a grand new house in the grounds to a unique design. Surmounted by minarets and embellished with many eastern features, it began to take shape in a style which Mrs Barrett described as being out of the 'Arabian Nights'. Inlaid mother-of-pearl in the mahogany doors, balustrades of brass, crimson flock wallpaper and delicately carved fireplaces brought lustre to the interior. It must have fascinated the growing family to watch its development over the seven years to its completion.

The old Georgian house was converted into a stable block and Edward Barrett turned his attention to landscaping the grounds around the new dwelling. An underground passage led into the gardens where an icehouse and hothouse were located; ponds were laid and filled; grottoes and cottages emerged during three interest-packed years. Meanwhile the family continued to grow, until eventually eight sons and three daughters filled the home.

During all of these busy, productive years the family seems to have been bound by strong cords of affection. What makes their story so fascinating is the absolute contrast in their home life at Hope End to that of the legendary years which were to follow in Wimpole Street.

Elizabeth seems to have held her place among them all with complete accord. She shared the boys' tutor, and her outstanding intelligence seems to have been quickly recognised and appreciated by her parents. At a time when few Victorians saw any merit in educating their daughters, Edward Barrett showed commendable interest in Elizabeth's development. Though she mothered some of the younger children from time to time, no pressure was put upon her to take a domestic role in the household. A room was provided for her at the top of the house so that she could read undisturbed (even novels were not discouraged), continue to study unhindered, and maintain her strong fascination with Greek translation. She also developed her talent for writing verse, which had emerged when she was about nine years old with birthday odes for members of the family.

Her father's loving interest remained constant despite the advent of eight stalwart sons. There was never a 'nose out of joint' experience for Elizabeth. His first letter to her (just before the move into Hope End) begins 'My dear Puss' and that cosy warmth seems to have been maintained over the years. In her early teens she pleaded to be allowed to have a week with him in London and addressed him as 'My dearest, dearest Puppy'. She did not then succeed in getting what she wanted but her spontaneous mode of addressing him shows how approachable he was at that time. Indeed all the children loved him. According to Margaret Forster's lively biography of Elizabeth, a birthday message to his father was sent by the Barretts' seventh son (appropriately named Septimus) saying 'You are a funny old fellow and I hope you will be as funny when you are a nice old man and play with me at Grand Mufti.'

That Edward Barrett was also much loved by his wife is beyond question. Margaret Forster's book quotes her as exclaiming on one of his returns from London: 'Never was he more welcome. We sat down directly to our soup and chicken and half an hour basking in the armchair before a blazing fire, enabling him to get thro' the evening very comfortably roasting chestnuts till the rioters all went to bed. . .' There could not have been a happier household in Victorian England at that time. The picture they present is that of a truly united, lively family, far more emancipated than the average Victorian household.

Though the family home was hidden away from public gaze, its members were not discouraged from mixing with local families of suitable status, or from taking an interest in politics. Their father was a champion of democracy and Parliamentary Reform. His brother Samuel had recently become an MP and Edward himself was elected a High Sheriff of Herefordshire. By then he felt he could share his feelings on democracy and freedom with his eldest two children, though he does not seem to have recognised the incongruity of still owning slaves on his Jamaican plantation! Elizabeth absorbed ideas about the plight of the poor and downtrodden which were later to feature in some of her best poems, even though it does not seem to have touched her personal relationships.

On her 14th birthday Mr Barrett generously published an ambitious poem which had occupied Elizabeth for two years past, entitled *The Battle of Marathon*. To see her work in print was a marvellous boost to Elizabeth's conviction that her future lay in literature and hopefully this sustained her during a year-long undiagnosed illness which came on immediately afterwards. Spinal trouble was suspected and treated at Gloucester with no expense spared, and Elizabeth returned to Hope End to resume writing and sending work to various magazines. Nevertheless it was not until her 20th birthday that another volume was published – an even more ambitious work entitled *An Essay on Mind*. Though it had to be financed by a close friend of her mother's family, it served to gain her recognition in literary circles. Fourteen shorter poems included in the book made a wider appeal than the essay. The family was exuberant on publication day, the excitement spreading even to the nursery. Backed up and publicised by grandparents on both sides of the family, the initial 50 copies were soon sold.

Congratulations from a stranger brought a curious friendship into Elizabeth's life. Hugh Boyd was a blind Greek scholar and poet in his late forties living with his wife and daughter in Malvern. Elizabeth persuaded her reluctant father (though by now she was 22 years old) to allow her to visit Boyd, but soon the visits increased in regularity. Love of literature was undoubtedly the basis of their rapport but soon Elizabeth developed a strong personal feeling for the blind scholar which disturbed her parents. It was uncharacteristic of her. Sometimes she would start out so early that she arrived at Boyd's home before he was even shaved and made ready for her to read Greek to him and discuss work of mutual interest. Such energy and outreaching enthusiasm contrasts strangely with her future as the languid invalid on her couch in Wimpole Street who later won the heart of Robert Browning, and there is no conclusive evidence as to what brought about the transition.

Then a bombshell fell on the household at Hope End which minimised all other worries. Four years after the birth of her last child, Mary Moulton Barrett fell ill and died. Her death was totally unexpected and a shattering blow to her husband, who received the news in his London office.

The news brought Edward hastening home to Hope End, stifling his own grief to solace his children. Mrs Barrett was buried in nearby Ledbury and on her father's return Elizabeth saw how deep was his grief despite the spiritual counsel given to his children – his assurance that their mother's was 'a true saving faith'. Always close to him, 'Ba' (he always used her pet name) drew closer still and was convinced that she would never leave him while he lived. Yet even she could not fill that awesome gap which seemed too deep for the 43 year old widower to bear. Perhaps it was from that devastating day that 'the iron entered his soul'.

The family remained at Hope End for another four years, though life could never be the same again. Their mother's gentle presence had probably never been recognised so clearly as when it had gone. Elizabeth continued her writing in the room at the top of the house. She also recommenced her visits to Hugh Boyd once the first shock of grief was under control.

New burdens fell upon Edward Barrett. The Jamaican estates were less profitable as the slaves prepared for emancipation, and eventually he had to face the fact that to sell Hope End was inevitable. It was a terrible wrench. Designing and building it had been a dream fulfilled. He had loved the retreat from business into a different world. It was sad also for the children to part with the home their mother had created for them – the safe, predictable world of childhood. Most of them had been born there.

When departure time came, Elizabeth went with mixed feelings. She sympathised with her father's predicament and it so happened that the Boyds had been making signals that they, too, were moving from the West Country. She had realised by then that life must take a new turn and that the blind poet had nothing like the deep feeling for her that she expected of him. She still had her beloved books and her writing career. Wherever the family settled she resolved to lead her own life, undisturbed, in her own domain. It may be that in future years she wrapped herself in a cocoon of invalidism to ensure this.

And yet, for Elizabeth the future was to bring fame, exciting literary friendships, romance and marriage with Robert Browning, foreign travel and motherhood. The world then and now would puzzle over the enigma of her father's personality and the precise nature of her own ill health. Diaries and letters which have emerged in recent years seem to indicate that her father may have been too harshly judged by earlier writers. But the fact remains that 'Ba' was never forgiven by him for her stealthy marriage and departure from the family home, despite her many efforts to heal the breach. When he died in 1857 he was brought back to Ledbury, to the parish church of St Michael and All Angels with its slender detached spire, to be laid alongside his two Marys – his one true love and the four year old daughter who was her namesake. It was probably the last visit of the Moulton Barretts.

Elizabeth died only four years later. She was 55 years old and was buried in the Protestant cemetery in Florence, the city where she had enjoyed 16 happy years with Robert Browning. She had achieved fulfilment and fame, particularly with her last works completed in Italy, *Aurora Leigh* and *Sonnets from the Portuguese*. Her work, often touched by sombre undertones, has appealed to scholars at home and abroad. But the simple lines she penned about Herefordshire reveal the significance to her of the 23 formative years she spent there:

> 'Green is the land where my daily steps
>   In jocund childhood played
> Dimpled close with hill and valley
>   Dappled very close with shade;
> Summer show of apple blossom
>   Running up from glade to glade.'

The Elizabeth Barrett Browning Library in the town centre is Ledbury's own tribute to her.

The Duke's Farewell

A horrendous storm swept over south-west England in the autumn of 1483 – the worst of the century. Violent winds, torrential rain and great floods brought chaos in their wake. The many rivers became a vast lake in the counties of Hereford and Worcester. The death toll, fear and devastation were appalling. But to one man – Henry Stafford, Duke of Buckingham, it brought a fearful personal dilemma. Ruin stared him in the face. In what was to be the last week of his life he sought desperately in the West Country to extricate himself and his family from the web of intrigue in which they were all caught. Only the sympathy and co-operation of the men of Herefordshire could deliver him and his from certain death.

From the small town (as it then was) of Weobley, he sent out an urgent summons to gentlemen living near his estates in the county, and sought to convince them that he had grave and genuine cause to repent of his former role as 'kingmaker' to the present ruler, Richard III, and had been entirely justified in joining Henry Tudor in his attempt to take Richard's throne from him. But now – with the supporting French fleet stormbound and battered in the Channel, while Welsh and British partisans were stranded amid the floods in Herefordshire, the rebellion had collapsed. The Duke was suddenly, terrifyingly, isolated.

He has been described as a man of sharp wit and rapier

intelligence. It would take every bit of those faculties to win support now. His listeners must have been spellbound as he poured out his tale, because the Duke was known to have been the bosom friend and greatest beneficiary of King Richard and had proudly followed him in the Coronation procession only three months before. Richard had piled honours and possessions (including those in Herefordshire) upon the Duke. Why, then, had he taken the terrible risk of biting the hand that fed him? Was it because the Duke, as High Constable of the realm, had been appalled at discovering the murder of the King's two nephews, the 'Princes in the Tower'? Or was there some other motive, some hidden purpose? The Herefordians were cautious.

But some of the Duke's hearers were convinced, or were moved with compassion at the plight of the family he had brought with him – his two sons and their mother. A family at Weobley took in the Duchess and Sir Richard Delabere of Kinnersley Castle bravely undertook charge of the two boys. If the story the Duke had told was true, and the King had been so merciless to his own nephews, it boded ill for the sons of the man now branded as a traitor. Hemmed in by the floods and the cordon which the King's troops had thrown around the area, the Duke remained a few days more in hiding and a copy of an old Roll dated 1575 reveals a touching glimpse of the family's last days together. Referring in particular to the Duke's elder child, it reads: 'My Lorde, his father, made him a Fryse coat, and at his departing he delivered his sonne and Heyre to Sir Richard Delabere Knight for to kepe until he sent for him by a token. . .' The 'Fryse coat' must have been a little jacket made in freize cloth, a rough woollen fabric having a shaggy nap on one side but with a smoother interior. The Duke's sudden transition from the corridors of power to spend nerve-wrecking hours in hiding must have discovered in him an unsuspected talent!

And so, having delivered up the boys, the Duke bade them farewell and fled in disguise, a hunted fugitive. Almost immediately came a proclamation from the King offering £4,000 reward for the discovery of the Duke, 1,000 marks for the eldest boy, and for the younger son, 'Lord Henrie', 500 marks.

To the Delabere's disgust their former friends, the Vaughans, searched assiduously, even in Kinnersley, but in vain. Shortly after this 'all the gent of Harreffordeshire', says the old record, 'were sent for by Privy Seal to King Richard' and there made the discovery that Duke Henry had been betrayed by one of his tenants in Shropshire and taken bound on horseback to Salisbury. Here he pleaded in vain for one last interview, face to face, with the royal cousin he had betrayed. What could he have hoped for? But on Sunday, 1st November, All Saints Day, the third Duke of Buckingham, himself of royal blood and in the line of succession, was condemned and executed after the striking off of his right hand to mark his treachery.

But in Herefordshire the drama was far from over. Before news of the Duke's death reached Kinnersley there came a messenger saying the Lord Stafford's father now wished his heir to be returned to him. Dame Elizabeth Delabere appears to have taken command of the situation and, being fore-warned, had disguised the boy 'in maiden's raiment' and smuggled him overnight to nearby Newchurch. She stoutly denied having the boy at Kinnersley and invited the messenger to search the castle. The man had to content himself on that occasion with a more successful forage at Weobley, where he traced the Duchess and took her to the king in London. The good Dame, together with her helper William ap Symon, then smuggled both boys back into the castle.

The next attempt to get the boys came with the news that Sir Richard Delabere was in the King's custody and there would remain unless the Buckingham heir was delivered! But once again their protectors had been forewarned and the children smuggled out of the castle to a hamlet then known as Adeley (later to become Ayley), where they hid for four days until they ran out of provisions. Again the castle was searched in vain. A few days later the sound of riders approaching sent Dame Delabere hurrying off into Kinnersley Wood, where she crossed the brook with the Buckingham heir 'in her lappe' and hid for four hours until the faithful Will ap Symon came to give the all clear.

It was now obvious that Kinnersley was too hot a place to hold the refugees and the hunted heir was dressed as a girl and put to ride side saddle behind Will ap Symon, to be conveyed to the house of a widow in Hereford. There both children remained safely hidden until better times – which, for them, came with the successful invasion of their father's ally, Henry Tudor, and his accession to the throne as Henry VII.

The story of Dame Delabere's loyal protection comes to life in the 1575 Roll which describes the side saddle escape of the heir 'upon a pillowe, like a Gentlewoman in Gentlewoman's apparell, and I wisse he was the fairest Gentlewoman, and the best ever she hadden in her daies or ever shall have, whom she prayeth daily to preserve him from his enemies and to send him good for time in grace.'

With such timely friendship, and his little frieze coat, hopefully the new Duke of Buckingham found comfort after that terrible time of retribution.

All
for
Love

❧

ROMANTIC novelists, jewellers and cosmetic salesmen all support the idea that the most desirable thing in life is — to be desired. But even that happy state has its pitfalls, as a fair damsel from the north east Herefordshire area of Edvin Ralph discovered to her dismay in the 14th century. Two young noblemen from neighbouring estates, Baron Ralph and Lord Y'Edvin, had been friends since youth but were parted for a while when Lord Y'Edvin decided to seek adventure by joining a Crusade to the Holy Land. When he returned, unharmed and self-confident through prowess in the Middle East, he fell in love with this lovely maiden who lived in a castle near his own home. Unfortunately his former friend, Baron Ralph, was paying court to the same lady, so bitter rivalry then ensued. How the object of their desire felt about it, and whether she showed encouragement to either of them is not revealed in the meagre details available. But matters came to a head one day when the Baron and His Lordship decided to end the indecision once and for all. One challenged the other to a duel in the meadow where no doubt, they had once played as lads together. It was to be fought to the death. Presumably this process of elimination would wonderfully concentrate the lady's mind.

On the appointed day the two swordsmen met in the meadow and selected a pitch which was close to the bridge leading to Buckenhill. They brought no supporters or witnes-

31

ses and intended to conduct the affair in secrecy. They attacked each other with savage fury — but the result was a total disaster. The tale is engagingly told in verse in *The Mournful Ballad of Baron Ralph and Lord Yedvin* which appeared in the *Bromyard News and Record* of April 19th 1931:

'Through the castle gate rode Baron Ralph,
    A haughty scan had he
In steel, if clad with axe and sword,
    And a lordly dignity.
He loved a lady of great beauty —
    A dark brunette to view —
And his anger was great for Lord Yedvin
    Did love that lady too.

A man of might was Lord Yedvin
    And many a far country
His valour had seen. In Palestine
    The infidel fought he.
To revenge their wrongs in single fight
    These Lordlings had agreed,
With none to see but Heaven above
    By a brook in a flowery mead.

The hour had come and swords were drawn
    And flashed in sunlight fair,
And steed t'wards steed impetuously
    They urged — that haughty pair.
Again and again in dreadful charge
    They met and hacked away,
Till in the hay both valorous knights
    Unhorsed in the meadow lay.

They rose again with sword in hand
   And at each on foot they flew,
Now parrying blow — now forward! back!
   And blood for blood they drew.
The lady saw all from her castle wall
   And swift as lover can,
Without a thought of her own dear life,
   To rescue from death she ran.

Without a thought she between them stood
   They fought, unheeding the maid
Till by wild mischance the swords of fate
   In that maid's breast were laid!
Then pause was held for a little space
   As her life blood ebbed away,
But when pale death on that face appeared
   To fight they again essay.

In feebler fight they grapple again
   For both were in woeful case;
They struggled on, but ere night appeared
   Were lying in death's embrace.
The next morn's light saw all three dead,
   But woeful was the sight,
And buried they were in Edvin's church
   At night by a keeper's light.

They reared to their memory statues three,
   The knights were in armour graved,
And age to age has the sad tale spread
   As the tombs have Time's tooth brav'd. . . .
And years ago at morning prime
   All near these faithful dead,
Did love-lord maids their orisons tell
   And priests their masses said.'

(Traditional)

How much of the tale is true and how much enhanced by poetic licence is difficult to establish after a lapse of six centuries. Sadly the poet's observation that the tombs had defied the march of time cannot now be justified. If any love-lorn maid of the twentieth century should wish to linger and ponder over these lovers' tombs she would be disappointed. Tombstones and statues in the delightful country churchyard two or three miles north of Bromyard have all decayed and have been resited. A number of crumbling memorial tablets have been re-erected against the outside walls of the church of St Michael's. But the lettering is indecipherable and the knightly statues which now lie under the tower inside the building cannot be positively associated with the tale, though a framed document alongside the Visitors' Book outlines and quite graphically illustrates the famous duel and its consequences.

The most practical and enduring memorial to the two combatants is that their names have been combined in this rural and peaceful locality which is known as Edvin Ralph. Strangely enough the lady whose charms stirred so much passion, and whose actions were surely the most heroic of the three, remains for ever a beautiful, anonymous shadow in the background.

Harmony
in
Monkland

MISS Laetitia Bonner must have been a young lady of
singular charm to have not one but two Herefordshire
vicars fall in love with her. She herself came of an Orleton
family and the vicar there found himself under threat of losing
the object of his affections when Henry Williams Baker, just
30 years old and heir to a baronetcy, arrived in the nearby
village of Monkland in 1851. It appears, however, that the
Rev W. Edwards won the day and led Miss Laetitia to the
altar of Orleton church.

Since history has little to record about the Rev Edwards
and his marriage, it is not possible to know whether the good
lady ever had any regrets. It is said that relations between the
two vicarages never became cordial, but Sir Henry Williams
Baker stayed on in the newly built Monkland vicarage for 25
very successful years and achieved some distinction through
his pastoral and social care there, and even more for his love of
sacred music. To the vicarage built to his design a private
chapel was added where his beloved organ was given an
honoured setting. It is pleasing to think of him seated there
after his disappointment in love, fingers lingering over the
keys while he consoled himself with comforting thoughts and
gentle harmonies, for he was something of a composer himself.
That he soon became reconciled to his single bliss is evidenced
by his hymn, written quite early in his life at Monkland, '*Oh,
what, if we are Christ's, is earthly shame or loss?*'. Indeed it seems

that so far from regretting his lost love, Sir Henry became a decided supporter of celibacy in the priesthood!

Cared for by his sister Jessy, five years younger than himself and very devoted to him, the bachelor vicar set about restoring the dilapidated church with the aid of a promising young architect, and building a school on a site freely given from his vicarage glebe land. Both projects received his financial backing, after which he turned his attention to the sphere he loved best – music, composing and song. Soon he was attracting kindred spirits from far afield and sister Jessy proved a capable and willing hostess of musicians who were not only sharing compositions, but amalgamating their own hymns and others into a book which became known and loved throughout England – *Hymns Ancient and Modern*. It included one compositon of Sir Henry's which became a firm favourite and for which his name became known and respected far beyond Monkland, '*Lord Thy word abideth, and our footsteps guideth*'. It was first sung at the reopening of his church after restoration.

The several distinguished men who joined Sir Henry in compiling *Hymns Ancient and Modern* became close friends, but perhaps none was more welcome at the vicarage than Professor W. H. Monk, who became musical editor of the anthology which occupied and delighted the group so much. Monkland village choir enjoyed the privilege of first performance when new tunes were tried out, and, inspired by their enthusiastic vicar, the villagers reached a very high standard. Simple folk, country born and bred, they would have welcomed their own vicar's compositions such as the one which emerged in 1868, '*The King of love my Shepherd is*'. It became familiar to thousands of schoolchildren in England in morning assembly after its debut in Monkland's new village school.

Professor Monk often played the fine organ at the beautifully restored church pastored by Sir Henry, enjoying the hospitality of the vicar and his sister. They must have had their affection for him sorely tried, however, when he showed scant regard for his friend's sermons. It is recorded by the Herefordshire writer Norman C. Reeves that he frequently fell asleep during that time and, moreover, snored audibly! How the vicar coped with his congregation under such circumstances we are not told, but with such a mirth-provoking diversion it is hardly likely that Sir Henry got the wrapt attention he deserved! But, happily for Monkland, his parishioners enjoyed a sense of great harmony in their relations with him. Church services were often crowded and in the rather stilted phraseology of the day the *Herefordshire Journal* later reported 'With every face he was familiar, sympathised with every suffering, joyed in every smile. . . .all who knew him were drawn to him by his simplicity and purity of character, and loved him with that love that casts out fear.'

In fact those words were part of the obituary which, alas, came far too soon for Sir Henry's distinguished musical friends and his parishioners. He died after a short illness, quite unexpectedly, in early 1877. His last parochial letter in the church magazine was addressed 'My dear friends and children in Jesus Christ', and the whole tone of the letter, though not intended as a farewell, indicates that though human family ties were denied him, Sir Henry was wedded to his parish and felt a deep parental concern for his flock.

More than a century later *Hymns Ancient and Modern* are still used in churches, and among them are the 'old favourites' requested often by TV viewers in such programmes as *Songs of Praise* and *Praise Be!*.

John O'Gwent

IT would be an extraordinary coincidence if Kentchurch Court provided sanctuary for *two* elderly reprobates in the second decade of the 15th century, to both of whom were ascribed magical powers and the doubtful privilege of being on bargaining terms with the Devil. So it seems possible – even probable – that Jack o'Kent and John o'Gwent were one and the same person.

The story goes that Jack o'Kent enlisted the aid of the Evil One in building a bridge across the river Monnow leading to Kentchurch. Since the Devil rarely gives favours for nothing, Jack promised that he should have the soul of the first one to go across the bridge after its completion. When that time came the artful Jack threw a bone over the bridge from one side to the other, and a hungry dog sped across into the path of the Devil!

So the story gives 'one up' to Jack o'Kent. But it seems that caution played a part in future dealings, for he is supposed to have stabled 'magic horses' in the cellar of Kentchurch Court against the need for any sudden flight. And when he neared the end of his earthly career he seems to have been rather uncertain about his soul's destiny. So he is said to have staged a competition between a dove (heaven bound) and a raven, the winner to claim his soul in death. And to make it easier for the two contestants he requested that the bait (his own liver and lights) should be impaled on the church steeple! This seems a very chancy way indeed for settling such an important issue, and there is no record of anyone attending his deathbed being inspired to carry out his request. So no one knows the fate which befell his mortal soul.

It is said that behind almost every legendary figure there is a real person on whom the story is based. Someone researching tales of Jack o'Kent glanced over parish records and found that the vicar of Kentchurch at that time was the Reverend John Kent. He posed the query: Could he have been Jack? To fit this theory the vicar would have had to live a Jekyll and Hyde existence. It seems much more likely that Jack was in fact John o'Gwent, who was also a lone wanderer around Kentchurch and whose real identity has never been in doubt. He was the father of the mistress of Kentchurch Court, Lady Scudamore – none other than Owen Glendower, the last great Welsh chieftain to harass the English from across the border. His name still carries the ring of romantic courage which brought men flocking behind his banner of the Red Dragon in the years of struggle against the English.

At the time of his daughter Alice's marriage to Sir John Scudamore it seems that there was peace on the border, and the Scudamores, among other Englishmen, were friends with their Welsh neighbours. Indeed Alice's marriage was followed by five of her sisters finding love among the English border families. Owen Glendower had not always been an enemy of the English. He was cultured, well travelled and had studied law in England. He had been called to the bar and made many aristocratic and influential friends. He was frequently at the Court of King Richard II. It seemed a golden era of peace with the Welsh. No wonder those romances had blossomed in Herefordshire!

So what turned this idyllic situation into more bloodshed and tragedy? It happened when King Richard II was ruthlessly deposed by his cousin Henry Bolingbroke, and ugly rumours were flying around that Richard had been – or would be – murdered. Owen fled back to his Welsh stronghold to summon support and perhaps save the abducted king and was immediately declared a traitor. The truce with the English was over! Owen would have no truck with the royal supplanter. Many English subjects shared his sense of outrage and joined him. For 15 years Owen fought and came near to gaining mastery over the whole of the West of England. But eventually the tide turned. Glendower's forces were finally vanquished, with the Herefordshire borderland ravaged and impoverished in the struggle.

Now, of course, Owen was branded a rebel and a wanted man by the English. His excursions into Kentchurch, and to his other daughter at Monnington Straddel, were stealthy and in disguise. It was vital that they should not be implicated, and the lone figure who issued forth, now as a shepherd, now as a minstrel, in Herefordshire's fields and lanes, gladly took refuge in the name of John o'Gwent. And, of course, like any mystery figure who seems to shun the company of 'locals', speculation was rife. To the villagers around he became a mystery man and a wizard. In the tales which were woven around the name of John o'Gwent, the story of the building of the Monnow Bridge comes to light again – but this time it was supposed to have been built by the mystery Welshman in one night with the aid of his familiar spirits. 'But,' adds a narrator, 'it could not have been through the evil one, for he never would have done so good an action.' A victory for common-sense. . .

But, of course, the tales persisted. Up comes the tale of magic horses again. For John o'Gwent, it was said, 'They traversed the air with the speed of Lapland witches.' As for the deathbed pact with the Devil, the version cast upon John o'Gwent was as fanciful as that ascribed to Jack o'Kent. John is supposed to have obtained his miraculous powers by barter-ing his soul to the devil, with the proviso that it would only be claimed if he should be buried either inside or outside the church. That particular tale ends by claiming that John o'Gwent had the guile to be buried beneath the east window of the church in Kentchurch – under the wall – so that he was half in and half out! It would be comforting to think that the Devil could be out-manoeuvred by human wit. Actually, no one really knows where Glendower died.

Kentchurch Court still stands with its old traditions and reminders of those epic days 600 years ago. The stables which housed those 'magic horses' have survived into the 20th century and would seem to indicate that the animals were sufficiently earthbound to require normal stabling. The panel-led room in which Owen slept (when it was safe to do so) still survives. The tower named after him stands as a sturdy monument to the faithful surveillance observed by the Scudamore household in 1415. Their vigilance saved the old warrior from the indignity of capture and all the horrors which might well have followed. Giving sanctuary in time of need adds a certain grace to any distinguished house. It does so for Kentchurch Court.

Remedies
and
Rhymes

IT might be supposed that Herefordshire folk are exceptionally healthy if judged by the tale of a Serjeant Hoskyns who was host to King James I at Morehampton Court, Abbey Dor. For entertainment he presented a group of Morris Dancers whose average age numbered 100 years. For one or two healthy citizens to reach that age may not constitute a record, but for several centenarians to be so nimble of foot must be remarkable. But the tale is narrated in a number of old records as if it were fact and not fiction.

Nevertheless the county had its share of ills and chills and some remedies used in the distant past give rise to the thought that the cure was worse than the complaint. Dr Gaston's remedy for 'Belly Ake' recounted in Symonds' Diary seems almost benign. It included 'brimstone beaten to a powder, black sope to make a paste, and give him the quantity of a hen egg; stirr him and keep him warme.'

Karen Wallace, who has published a delightful book on *Herefordshire Foods*, unearthed a handwritten copy of Elizabeth Foley's recipe book of 1693 which claims: 'An excellent thing to bring a man to life when he is fallen into a fitt of apoplexy. Fry a bag of salt and place it, still hot, on the stomach of the sufferer... A man was brought to life this way that had been dead for two days!'

On his parochial visits around the Bredwardine area, Francis Kilvert came across many sick folk and recounts their

The Sin Eater

experiences with sympathetic interest. A jaundice sufferer was given a mixture made from the inner bark of the barberry tree, boiled down into what would have been a yellowish fluid. This seems almost to suggest the homeopathic theory of 'like curing like'. Another parishioner suffered from the effects of water around the heart and was relieved of it by somehow getting it to run out of his heels! Fortunately mumps does not usually end by leaving the patient with lockjaw, but a lad who was so afflicted had to endure two months' treatment at Hereford Infirmary while his jaws were prised open by using a screw lever! What a mercy chloroform had already been invented and was made available to this youngster.

Medical aid was too costly for the working class during most of the 19th century and they were thankful for advice from the parish priest and older housewives, who could only speak from trial and error. Sulphur and hog's lard was prescribed for a boy suffering from 'the itch', which seems more acceptable than the remedy for curing a wen (cystic swelling) on the neck – to rub it with moles' blood. The old woman who recommended it insisted 'But ye must ha' faith', though in what or who is not made clear in the record.

For nettle stings the dock leaf was always available (the plants grow together as a rule). Many of us can endorse this from experience, even without repeating nine times over the chant:

'Out nettle, in dock,
In the name of the Father, Son, and Holy Ghost.'

But doubtless it helped to pass the time until the sting had subsided.

Burns and scalds came under the scrutiny of no less a one than the diarist Samuel Pepys, who prescribed merely the chanting of:

'There came three Angells out of the east,
The one brought fire, the other brought frost.
   Out fire, in frost,
In the name of the Father, Son, and Holy Ghost.'

45

It seems a curious admixture of prayer and concentrated wishing.

Other 'cures' called for some kind of charm or talisman – for a sore throat merely draping the patient's own stocking (from his or her *left* foot) around the patient's throat at bedtime sufficed. A ring, fashioned from a shilling taken out of the church offertory box, was supposed to cure fits. A loaf, baked on a Good Friday and marked with a cross, was expected to remain wholesome for a year and to provide a remedy for a variety of ills if powdered and given in water. Feeding a child from a bowl made of ivy wood was said to cure whooping cough; but during an epidemic at Blakemere an old woman declared that in her young days simply to take a child to the miller would suffice. He would set the mill in motion and repeat the familiar benediction:

'In the Name of the Father, Son, and Holy Ghost
I grind away this disease.'

and it was claimed to work every time.

However, the incantation prescribed for a mad dog's bite is quite mystifying, and would have been a strain on the larynx had it not been written on a piece of paper, for placing over the bite *with a morsel of cheese*! It ran . . .

'Frary, Guary, Nary. Guary, Frary, Nary. Nary, Frary, Guary.'

and was supposed to be infallible! Strange also was the cure for rupture at Eardisland – a willow tree with a hole through its hollow trunk through which a child could be passed by his father, on the one side, into the arms of a willing helper on the other. Since this act had to be performed nine times it was quite a ceremony, and was solemnized by the chant from the father: 'The Lord giveth', which was met from the other side with the response: 'The Lord receiveth'.

Herbal remedies must surely have provided a sounder basis for healing. They are time honoured. Figwort was popular for poultices and for healing cuts. The inner bark of the elder tree could be boiled with hops and drunk by sufferers from inflammation. One quaint way of finding the right herb with which to treat a patient was to look into a beryl (a small crystal) to see the likeness of the appropriate species of herb. Crystal gazing? Sir Edward Harley possessed such a beryl at Brampton Bryan. His mother, Lady Brilliana, was generous in her herbal recommendations to neighbours, but whether she used such an aid is not known. Her son's was a work of art, a perfect sphere, just an inch in diameter mounted on a gilt stem ten inches high with the names of four angels (Uriel, Raphael, Michael and Gabriel) engraved on the mounting. Such a combination of angelic helpers, crystal gazing, and field herbs seems to show the desperation of the sick to leave no stone unturned.

Doctors were beyond the pockets of the poor, and the Herefordshire writer H. L. V. Fletcher quotes a farmer as saying: 'I dunna worry the doctors much. I d'go to the chemist and ask him to mix me a real *strong* bottle. A real good 'un. That puts me right.'

Many a child in years gone by dreaded 'having the doctor' and associated the old chant:

> 'I do not love thee, Doctor Fell:
> The reason why I cannot tell,
> But this I know, and know full well
> I do not love thee, Doctor Fell.'

with the ominous appearance of a dark, bottled concoction which tasted vile. Dr Fell was a Herefordshire divine, living near Much Marcle in his youth, and later Dean of Christ Church College, Oxford, where he may have gained his unpopularity. It has been suggested to me that it was his students who composed the ditty because of his austerity and the difficulty of pleasing him. It is thought that he returned to Herefordshire (or adjoining Worcestershire) when he fell foul of the Roundheads and was turned out of his Deanery. His wife refused to go voluntarily and was eventually carried out on a plank, it is said! So, all in all, he may deserve our sympathy and not our censure.

People who lived in the Kingland area were fortunate in having Elizabeth Hughes for a neighbour. Round about 1800 it became known that she had 'the healing touch'. She was a simple, unlettered woman who could not even sign her name. She used no charms or superstitions but insisted that her own belief in the New Testament promise 'The prayer of faith shall save the sick' must be shared by the sufferers. She had critics among the intellectuals and a Hereford schoolmaster satirised her:

> 'Know this, ye sons of Credulity, know
> 'Tis faith alone can conquer every woe!
> Have faith in Mrs Hughes, to her abode
> Sons of Affliction, flee by ev'ry road!'

And so they did, from as far away as the south coast and the eastern counties. There's many a true word spoken in satire. Many were healed.

Sadly, of course, not every partaker of physic, herbs, or other help responded to the cures. In the last resort the next of kin was sometimes concerned for the cure of a man's soul and went to the length of calling in 'the sin eater'; a seemingly macabre ceremony, but one which was certainly employed on numerous occasions. Brand's *Antiquities* gives details of the hiring of some living person (a stranger preferred) to present himself at the place where coffin and mourners were assembled before the time of burial. He was detailed to stand on one side of the bier (or coffin) and the next of kin to stand opposite. A loaf of bread was produced and handed over the body of the deceased to the man who undertook to be the sinbearer, followed by a bowl of beer which he was bidden to drink. On payment of sixpence the 'sin eater' took upon himself the guilt of the late departed, ostensibly to free that soul from a troubled time hereafter. So seriously did the onlookers regard this that the 'sin eater' was chased away from the village with the utmost speed.

Destiny
and
Candlelight

CANDLEMAS Day of 1461 dawned bright, clear and bitterly cold. The iron-hard ground glittered with hoar frost as Owen Tudor took the road to Mortimer's Cross. He shivered but his mind was alert. This was the 40th anniversary of that spectacular Candlemas Day when he, with King Harry's victorious army, returned from France to a tumultuous welcome at Dover. Then Henry V was 34 years old, exuberant in his prime. He had restored England's fortunes in France and secured a profitable treaty with the French king. Moreover, to confirm his triumph and provide him with a serious claim to the French throne itself, he brought home a trophy in warm flesh and blood — the French king's daughter, Katharine of Valois. It was a fairytale come true and the English loved it — the conquering hero winning the hand of the king's daughter and bringing with her the spoils of love and war.

Owen Tudor's involvement in this romance and epic adventure had all begun when he first took this road from North Wales into Herefordshire to volunteer for King Harry's army. He was 15 years old, defying his guardian's wishes because he hungered for action and life outside the Welsh hill fortress. He had tired of life with the old men around his guardian and kinsman, Owen Glendower, of the frustrated dreams of the Welsh and of the brooding hatreds and feuds which had been his diet since childhood. So Owen crossed the border and

joined up with King Harry's troops. Six years on the bat-
tlefield amid slaughter and suffering had brought him to
manhood and into the royal household as a personal aide.

To Owen's immense surprise this domestic role had presented him with the greatest adventure of all. Within two
years the warrior king had died, a victim to plague. Little
Harry, nine months old, succeeded his father and the helpless
child was taken from his mother into the guardianship of his
ambitious uncles. While they jockeyed for power the widowed
Queen Katharine had turned to Owen for comfort, and before
long, for love!

In all the 40 years that had elapsed since that wonderful
Candlemas Day at Dover, the dozen years spent with Katharine had perhaps been the most momentous — and the most
dangerous. He and the dowager queen had lived on the edge
of fear because there were rules governing an alliance with a
king's widow. Owen would be regarded as a Welsh upstart
despite his claim to descent from the old Welsh rulers, so his
life with Katharine had been shrouded in secrecy — until his
sons were born. Then the secret was out, but it was not until
36 year old Katharine's death that the reckoning had come.
Then Owen had been thrown into Newgate Prison.

But happily, when young Harry came of age to govern,
Owen was pardoned, his sons legitimised and given titles by
their kingly half-brother. Edmund had become Earl of Rich-
mond and Jasper, Earl of Pembroke, and from then on had
served young Harry well in the civil war which had sprung up
through the Duke of York's rebellion and claim to Harry's
throne. Edmund had lost his life in that cause but thankfully
Jasper still lived and was now in step with his father, crossing
Herefordshire with an army of 8,000 they had raised in Wales!
Soon they would cross the Severn to join the rest of the
Lancastrian king's army and, if this 40th anniversary of
Candlemas was a sign of good fortune, put down the Yorkist
rebellion for good and all. The Duke of York and his eldest son
had already lost their lives in the struggle, but it was
rumoured that his second son, Edward the Earl of March, had
risen to avenge his father and brother, and to pursue York's
claim to the throne.

The Tudors pressed on across the rich meadows which had once been part of Wales. An east wind greeted them as they neared Mortimer's Cross. The name might have had a melancholy ring but Owen knew that it was only so named because it marked the crossroads to the east and the north. By now, he reflected, all godfearing young women who had given birth in the past twelve months would be preparing their candles for the celebration at the parish church of the Vigil of the Virgin Mary. Soon, holding their lighted candles, they would move in to receive cleansing and sanctification – a time honoured custom. It had endured in England for a thousand years, this holy day of gentle piety. Owen resolved that the troops should pass through as orderly as possible.

Suddenly the air was rent with a terrifying cacophony of sounds – the shrieks of men and horses and the unmistakable clash of weapons! It was nine o'clock in the morning and the young Earl of March had descended on the crossroads from his mother's castle of Wigmore, four miles to the north, and flung an army of 11,000 to intercept the Welsh. The Tudors and their men had been ambushed. They fought desperately, but hemmed in by the river Lugg on one side and encircled by exultant enemies who had not exhausted themselves by marching since daybreak, the odds were overwhelming. And as if the weapons of surprise and superior numbers were not sufficient, the strapping young Earl of March (19 years old and six ft four inches tall) suddenly and dramatically claimed divine aid through a 'sign in the sky' – the appearance of three suns overhead. They represented the three remaining sons of the slain Duke of York, Edward claimed, and were shown to rise in splendour!

So it was not only the imaginative Welsh who looked for signs, wonders and wizardry. The triple sun has since been recognised as a natural occurrence, often brought about by the formation of ice crystals in the upper air. But the vision of the three suns will forever be linked in our history books with the overwhelming victory of the new young Duke of York at Mortimer's Cross. It is said that 4,000 men lay dead on the Herefordshire farmlands between Wigmore and Kinsham, and that many poor countryfolk gathered spoils from those who would need their goods no longer. It is, after all, an ill wind that blows nobody good!

Somehow Jasper Tudor managed to escape and fled back to Wales, but among the prisoners rounded up on that sad day was 62 year old Owen. He was among the ten men sentenced by the triumphant Duke Edward to face the block which was being prepared in Hereford's Market Place. It was a compliment of sorts for the man who had once been dubbed by the English as a Welsh upstart. Edward claimed that he always spared the common soldiers, sentencing to death only the lords and men of influence.

When the prisoners arrived at Hereford the stage was set. The crowd of townsfolk noisily jostling for ringside places eyed Owen curiously and with some hostility it appears. The historian Gregory writing his *Chronicles* not long after the event, shows little feeling for the victim when describing the scene. 'Owen Tudor was weening and trusting all the way that he should not be beheaded till he saw the axe and the block, and when that he was in his doublet he trusted on pardon and grace till the collar of his red velvet doublet was ripped off. Then he said "That head shall lie on the stock that was wont to lie on Queen Katharine's lap", and put his heart and mind wholly unto God, and full meekly took his death.'

After death, Owen Tudor was awarded the doubtful honour of having his still handsome features raised on a stake above the other heads. But there is an affecting sequel to the tale which has been handed down in history – that 'a mad woman combed his hair and washed away the blood from his face, and she got candles and set about him more than a hundred.'

That circle of lighted candles formed a crown. Owen's red-haired little grandson, Henry Tudor, was destined to be the Welshman who would rule over England and bring her peace, stability and prosperity.

Owen Tudor had founded a dynasty.

Lady Brilliana
Under Siege

FOR several hundred years the Harleys were a powerful and influential family in North Herefordshire. They owned the two castles of Wigmore and Brampton Bryan and were highly respected, enjoying the friendship of well-to-do neighbours, administering their farms and generally managing their affairs with competence, with an eye to the welfare of the country folk around them. The head of the family during the reign of Charles I was Sir Robert Harley, the Member of Parliament for Hereford. He acquitted himself well at Westminster and seemed set to keep up the long reputation of the Harleys for outstanding leadership.

Sir Robert's excellent marriage with the daughter of Viscount Conway established a family relationship that was to turn his castle into a home as well as a fortress. The Hon. Brilliana (her title in her own right) has been described by the Rev Compton Reade MA – an enthusiastic and scholarly historian – as 'this glorious woman... one of the staunchest among the heroines of the Civil War.' Yet she was no Amazon, motivated by zeal for one side or the other. She has been described also as being delicate and refined, her portrait revealing 'an intelligent lustrous eye' in a sweet oval face, with a firm yet smiling mouth. Her slight figure was carried with a purposeful bearing. Her devotion and sense of responsibility to her children is evidenced in the letters which she wrote to her eldest son in times of separation.

Life was good at Brampton Bryan Castle until the terrible time when Parliament came into open conflict with the King. Most of Herefordshire pledged loyalty to His Majesty but the

Harleys believed they must seek the greater good of the country by standing out against Charles Stuart's misrule and the bad influence of the coterie surrounding him.

When it became clear that the King would never come to terms with his Parliament, Sir Robert was summoned to take up arms against him. He did so knowing he must leave his family at home unprotected and without even the comfort of friends and neighbours, who all supported the King. But before leaving home Sir Robert dismantled their second home at Wigmore Castle and brought goods and staff to join the family at Brampton Bryan. Bidding Lady Brilliana to hold the castle against any attack by the Royalists, he and his son Ned rode away, desperately hoping the conflict would be resolved before his home and family came under threat.

But the fighting was bitter and long. Fortunes of war fluctuated. Towns and garrisons changed hands with bewildering consequences. When Hereford was taken by the Royalist army, just a few miles away, the Brampton Bryan family knew that crisis time was at hand. A day of prayer and petitioning 'for the mercy of God to avert the dreadful judgment' was actually in progress when the dreaded blow fell on 25th July 1643. Sir William Vavasour and Colonel Lingen (former friends of the Harleys) marched against Brampton Bryan Castle and demanded admittance in the name of King Charles.

With but a half dozen troopers, a few scared neighbours, her small children, servants and farmworkers around her, the mistress of the castle summoned what composure she could against 600 Royalist troops. 'My lord bids me hold out!' was the reply she sent by her messenger. To prove they were in earnest, the besiegers claimed one victim in the street outside, 'an aged blind man', reported a contemporary historian, who added that the family's cook was then shot by a poisoned bullet 'which murdered him with great torment and poysomness to the whole family'. It was calculated cruelty to arrange that the poor cook was sent back to die before the terrified garrison, such as it was.

Sir John Harley's 800 sheep, 30 cows, oxen and other farm animals, together with 30 breeding mares and horses, were all confiscated and taken away. As if the empty pastures and dwindling household supplies were not intimidating enough, the Royalists then poisoned the fountain and the spring which supplied the locality, ravaged the church, destroyed the parsonage and homes of the villagers, burned buildings and outhouses of the castle and took themselves outside the town to destroy the mill. Each move would have been punctuated by a renewed challenge to the beleaguered household and a sadly repeated refusal to surrender. But the tension, from time to time, must have been immense.

Then in October, as suddenly as they appeared, the besiegers went. News reached them that their leaders had been driven out of Hereford and they themselves were in danger. For Lady Brilliana, the first glad relief was all too soon submerged at the sight of the devastation around the castle, at the ruined families who had been robbed, the starving poor who would have no stores to fall back upon, and the barbarous sacrilege of the church and parsonage. She was worn out with anxiety over her husband and son. Her deliverance had come at the expense of a reversal in the Parliamentary fortunes. So how now would the Harley fighting men fare? The future was filled with uncertainty and a wracking anxiety.

Sadly, the courageous woman at the centre of what has been described as 'one of the bravest deeds throughout the war', collapsed shortly after the siege was lifted. The fatigue, hardships and the terrible realisation of the full cost to others of her stand against the Royalists were more than she could bear. She was not strong physically. To the great grief of all around her, her life flickered out in the castle which had been saved at such cost.

For the gallant defender the struggle was over, but her family had many hurdles yet to clear. In 1644, other Royalist troops returned to Brampton Bryan, took prisoner the small garrison and the Harleys' three children and destroyed the castle! It must have been a heart-breaking homecoming for Colonel Sir Robert Harley and Captain Edward, even though by then their side had won the war and Parliament was ruling England. The Harleys were granted compensation for their terrible losses, and for those of the village who had also suffered, through an Order which empowered them to sequestrate from the estate of the Royalist who had fought against Brampton, Colonel Lingen.

But while these mundane matters were being sorted out, Sir Robert was going through the terrible trauma of feeling the sacrifice had been in vain! He became utterly disillusioned with the rule of Oliver Cromwell. Like many others who had fought against the king, he concluded that the abuse of power by Cromwell was greater than that of the king they had deposed and executed! The feeling between Harley and Cromwell intensified and when the Protector died on 3rd September 1658 a great storm raged through Brampton Bryan Park, destroying shrubs and trees. Legend has it that Sir Robert declared Cromwell was being dragged through by the Devil en route for Hell! And tradition claims that the Devil returns on each anniversary.

Francis Kilvert
Country Parson

THE diaries of Francis Kilvert, the now famous Herefordshire clergyman, are a wonderful introduction to the lives
of ordinary people in the 1870s.

Mary Price, for instance, who was mentally handicapped,
was in her mid fifties when the country vicar made his
parochial visit to the cottage which she shared with her
stepmother Priscilla. His accounts provide an illuminating
glimpse into country life in the village of Bredwardine in
Victorian times. The very simplicity of the writer's prose
recreates the calm unhurried atmosphere in which the two
women were sitting over tea when he arrived at the door.
Their story unfolds without embellishment, sentimentality or
moralizing.

Priscilla (Prissy) Price, in her late seventies, was clearly a
practical and knowledgeable parishioner who ventured to give
her vicar advice on the problem of administering a charity
fund. With no thought of seeking aid herself, she observed
sanguinely 'This charity interferes with people and does them
harm. Those who get it are discontented and those who don't
get it are discontented, but don't distress yourself.' So much
for Victorian attempts at welfare!

Limited as her faculties were, Mary must have sensed her
predicament should she outlive her kindly guardian — or
maybe she had overheard the sighing lament of some indis-
creet neighbour. In June 1878 she seemed to have developed a
kind of death wish. She greeted the vicar by pressing her hand
to her side and ejaculating 'Puff, Puff', which Priscilla ex-
plained was premonition of death. Mary followed on by

uttering a solemn 'Bom, Bom', and it did not take much imagination to recognize the sound of the great bell tolling over a graveyard. 'Then', says the diarist, Mary 'rose and curtsied profoundly', which Prissy pronounced as indicating how after death she would rise and curtsey to all who had been good to her. Suiting actions to the words — or gestures — Mary took herself down to the village carpenter, paid him a halfpenny and ordered her coffin.

But, sadly, when the big bell tolled — and it was Christmas Day of all days — it tolled for little Davie Davies, the shepherd's boy from nearby Old Weston. Even while the vicar carried mince pies and Christmas pudding to the Prices to celebrate yet another Christmas together, the shepherd's home was devastated by their unexpected loss.

Hastening to the family the vicar found the shepherd deeply distressed and bitter at the doctor's failure to save Davie. But the child's gentle mother appreciated the vicar's attempts to comfort them and took him upstairs to see Davie on his bed, looking for all the world like a child in sleep with dark curls resting on his pillow. For Kilvert and the mother this brought some comfort. But both were even more affected by the account Margaret Davies gave of the strange experience which came to Davie before he died: 'He saw a number of people and some pretty children dancing in a beautiful garden and heard some sweet music. Then someone seems to have called him for he answered "What do you want with me?" He also saw beautiful birds and the men of Weston (who later carried him to his funeral). He thought his little sister Margaret was throwing snow and ice on him.'

Snow fell on the coffin two days later. It was, in fact, blowing a near blizzard when the sad party assembled in church on Christmas Day at 2.15. 'Even the Welcome Home, as it chimed softly and slowly to greet the little pilgrim coming to his rest, sounded bleared and muffled through the thick, snowy air,' recorded the vicar. Somehow he managed to connect his sermon 'There was no room for them in the inn' with the little bed in the churchyard. Perhaps it was not surprising that the shepherd could not be comforted then or several days later when Kilvert met him in the twilight calling his sheep. Even so, the vicar bravely spoke to him of 'the Good Shepherd who had gathered his lamb with His arm and carried him to His bosom.'

Throughout the early weeks of 1879 Francis Kilvert continued his conscientious visitation and other parish duties despite being troubled with a chest infection and neuralgia. Life for him was very full. He had many friends of his own calling and mixed comfortably in the society of his better off parishioners from time to time. He enjoyed writing verse and had the occasional pleasure of seeing his work in print. Bredwardine vicarage was his first real home since boyhood and he took delight in furnishing it and equipping it with domestic staff, for in this momentous year he was to venture into matrimony.

Elizabeth Anne Rowland came from Woodstock, near Blenheim Palace. In earlier years his diaries had included romantic entries about other girls for whom he had formed attachments, though all seemed to come to nothing and he was disappointed. A curate with no settled home offered little inducement to the stern Victorian parents of that day and his mid thirties passed without prospect of domestic bliss. But in 1879 the die was cast. Tantalisingly, pages of the Diary during this period have been lost or removed, but the Herefordshire press gave good coverage to the marriage on 20th August that year, and the return from honeymoon in mid-September. The wedding had taken place in Woodstock, of course, so the Welcome Home was the Bredwardine contribution to the happy event. Cheers and banner-waving greeted the carriage as soon as the newlyweds came into sight, and a series of floral and evergreen arches led to the vicarage garden. Here tables were laid out covered with snow white cloths and tea-time delicacies. Clergy friends from around the area and county families combined to serve the villagers. Gifts were joyfully presented and celebrations continued, despite rainfall, into the evening to mark the happiest day Bredwardine had known for many years.

Ten days later the unbelievable happened. Francis Kilvert died of an illness which had given little cause for alarm on his return but which apparently moved to a sudden climax over the following weekend. Peritonitis is named as the cause. Friends throughout Herefordshire, over the border into Wiltshire (his parents' home) and along the Welsh borderland of his former parishes, were shocked and many devastated.

On the following Saturday, under a sky overcast with clouds, eight grieving parishioners assembled at the vicarage to carry their pastor the 60 yards to church. The vicar's father who had conducted the previous Sunday's services on behalf of his son, Dora — his sister and former housekeeper, three other sisters and a brother, joined the widow whose happiness had been so brief. Farmers, foresters, cottagers and schoolchildren made up the cortege under the widespread, wet foliage of the old cedar tree, beneath which tables had been spread just a fortnight earlier amid such high hopes. Some half dozen clergymen shared the sad ceremony in church and the vicar was borne to his grave near the pathway which led from the road to the church portals. Wreaths were gently placed alongside and weeping schoolchildren tossed wild flower posies onto the oak coffin bearing the inscription 'Robert Francis Kilvert, died Sept 23rd 1879, aged 38'.

It would have given him great pleasure to know that his published diaries became so celebrated and that his lovely prose descriptions of the countryside of Herefordshire and its borders were received with much pleasure by those who lived there and by others around the world. How could anyone set aside the country parson who wrote:

'I never had a lovelier journey up the lovely valley of the Wye. A tender, beautiful haze veiled the distant hills and woods with a gauze of blue and silver and pearl. It was a dream of intoxicating beauty. I saw the old familiar sights, the broad river reach at Boughrood flashing round the great curve in the sunlight over its hundred steps and rock ledges, the luxuriant woods which fringe the gleaming river lit up here and there by the golden flame of a solitary ash . . .'

His 38 years were good years and Herefordshire is the richer because of them.

Feasting with Fungi

THE 4th of October 1877 was literally a Field Day for the Woolhope Naturalists' Club, which had been founded 26 years earlier 'to promote the practical study of all branches of natural history and archaeology'. The Club still flourishes and is indeed a source of prestige to the county.

So famous had it become even in 1877 that visitors had applied from as far afield as the Continent, the Far East and New South Wales to join members and kindred spirits from other parts of Britain on their autumn 'fungus foray'. Surprisingly it was the mycological (fungi studying) branch of the Club which attracted publicity in the national press and probably alerted overseas naturalists and botanists to the activities in Herefordshire. The spongy 'morbid excrescence' was sought after as if for long lost treasure by this elite company of doctors, parsons, government officials, lawyers and other professional men. It is surely true that one man's meat is another man's poison!

The October 1877 foray was a four-day event culminating in a dinner at Hereford's Green Dragon Hotel, at which certain field discoveries were to be both commemorated and (literally) consumed after suitable treatment by the hotel chef.

But first the company of foragers had to converge from far and near to join Woolhopeans and to be entertained to dinner on the first night in the home of Dr Bull, a leading member who was a Hereford physician. Never, says the report published later, had there been so many overseas visitors at one event, but club members rested confident in their ability to communicate freely because Dr Bull spoke all languages (dead and living) with equal fluency! All of the club members were distinguished gentlemen, successful in their various professions, but in Dr Bull they were exceedingly fortunate. Moreover, he was a genial host and soon put everyone at ease. During his absence from the table for a few moments it transpired that no one present could recall either the French, Latin or Greek for 'Welsh Rabbit'. Hopefully the foreigners took it on trust, as they later did the strong brew of Foxwhelp cider, and tongues were suitably loosened.

All sympathised when an apology was read from the Rev J. E. Vize who, sadly, was detained in Montgomeryshire for two whole days because 'two persons in that benighted district had the bad taste to wish to be married during the week of the foray!' News came from Japan that next year the Mikado and three botanists from Yokohama hoped to join the autumn foray to seek some better method of producing the Shu-take fungus than their present one of tapping the Shu tree with a mallet. (It seems that no one in 1877 thought it at all odd that the ingenious Japanese needed Herefordshire advice on such an operation.) Monsieur de Seynes had brought with him from Central France not only his son and heir but also some magnificent specimens of the orange-topped fungus which, he assured the gathering, was the very species that was cooked under the direction of Agrippina and used to poison Claudius. No Woolhopean had seen it before and it was eagerly sketched into local notebooks.

Because the tracing and cooking of edible fungi was part of the foray programme, it was reassuring that instruction sheets were available showing how to recognise poisonous fungi. And for the unwary it was good to hear that antidotes were to be found in both oil and milk, which would serve to prevent the poison gripping the lining of the stomach – and that brandy provided a reviver.

The following three days exploration in woods and fields yielded a variety of experiences. Transport had to be provided to get to each location in good time for an early start. On the first day it was observed that one of the coach horses provided proved to be 'a desperate kicker who eyed the clergyman on the box in a most spiteful manner'. Had it been Monsieur Cornu seated there the animal might have been more justified, for the Frenchman brought out some impressive equipment from his own country – a big cylindrical vasculum and an instrument with a blade more than a foot long! Doubtless his companions resolved when on foot to give the Frenchman plenty of elbow room. On a later excursion (this time to Whitfield) transport was short and it was necessary to use two 'rank jibbers' (whatever they may have been) and four jet black undertaker's horses with flowing manes, long tails and a funereal trot. But one way and another all the eager foragers arrived at the scene of their explorations, which were rewarded by a fund of good humour and success.

Many rare Herefordshire fungi were detected in open ground, and a Puff-ball (officially *Lycoperdon gemmatum*) was found climbing the mossy side of a nearby tree. The discovery of the fungus 'Eye-bright' was recognised by the Frenchmen as 'Break-Spectacles' in their country. A more exciting find was a crimson-topped Agaric which, until its gills were thoroughly examined, was thought to be an already known species. But, finally ackowledged by all to be a new find, it was reverently packed away to be labelled and displayed as their 'first day trophy'.

It is obvious that much more goes on at ground level than most mortals are aware of. By this animated company, fungi seem almost to have been invested with personality. Treading through a tall common moss, Monsieur Cornu spotted a yellow mycelium, which he declared to be a parasite threading its way through and beneath the moss in search of its underground victim – the truffle. Others joined him in his detection work amongst the moss, and by following the trail of the mycelium the Frenchman was highly gratified when the hidden truffle came to light. The subject of truffles became even more fascinating when it transpired that there was competition between the said yellow mycelium on the one hand and squirrels and mice on the other.

So the lively, energy-demanding days progressed until time

for the closing event – dinner at the Green Dragon in Hereford. A beautifully designed menu was decorated with an illustrated border cleverly depicting names of well known fungiologists, some of whom were present. Seventy one diners sat down to the repast – all menu items were in French which perhaps made the astonishing variety of them even more impressive. It was a pity there occurred a misprint in the word which headed the fish course, the typesetter having left out the second 's' in the French word 'Poissons'. Nevertheless a good time was had by all and a special novelty was the fungus cooked and named in honour of Monsieur Cornu – *Craterellus cornucopiodes*. When cooked and served it turned jet black and resembled burnt onions! But its odour was inviting and the taste declared to be truly delicious.

Final speeches rounded off a highly successful Fungus Foray. The last paper presented by Dr Cooke carried the intriguing title 'What is the use of Fungus Hunting?', which was thoroughly enjoyed even though falling on the ears of the already converted.

What emerges quite clearly from the annual report in the club's 'Transactions' is that though these learned gentleman pursued their objectives so keenly, they were not devoid of understanding and patience with the uninitiated, nor did they lack the healthy leaven of humour. On a Gala Day in Hereford to which they must have been contributing some item, they were among the first to smile at the poster which irreverently described them as 'Fungus Fogies'. For them the rallying cry in verse was far more pertinent:

'Men of thought! be up and stirring night and day.
  There's a fount about to stream,
  There's a light about to beam,
  There's a warmth about to glow,
Funguses can joy bestow
More than common minds can know!
Men of thought and men of action
Here can find full satisfaction.'

Princess Alfrida's Tragic Love

ALFRIDA, daughter of the famous King Offa, must have been delighted when told that a neighbouring king had asked for her hand in marriage. All the signs are that she made little secret of her elation and aroused some very un-maternal reactions in the mind of her mother, Queen Quen-drida, who had become quite accustomed to life as the wife of the most powerful ruler in Britain in the year AD 792.

King Offa's kingdom of Mercia was the largest in Britain, extending from the Dyke in the west across to the coastal kingdom of East Anglia. As good fortune would have it, it was from that very kingdom that the proposal of marriage to Offa's daughter had come. It may well be that the exceptio-nally good character of their prospective son-in-law, and the future happiness of their daughter, weighed rather less in the minds of the parents than did the prospect of an alliance between their two adjoining kingdoms.

So the proposal was warmly received and messengers de-spatched to the young King Ethelbert inviting him to come to the palace of Offa to wed Princess Alfrida without delay. According to Capgrave's *New English Legends*, Ethelbert was not a man to do anything in haste. He was a very sober, upright fellow with a strong spiritual bent. It had been on the advice of his courtiers that he agreed to seek a bride and produce a successor to the East Anglian throne. They wanted him to try for the hand of Seledrith, who had already inherited her father's southern kingdom, but he set his heart upon Offa's daughter and theirs has all the signs of a genuine romance. The bride-to-be began to sing her lover's praises, boast of his good looks and nobility, and (perhaps unwisely) to predict that he would become more illustrious than her father!

Queen Quendrida's indulgence in listening to this happy, maidenly prattle did not last very long. It was ridiculous of course. Gentle, unambitious men like Ethelbert did not conquer their neighbours and become supreme rulers – unless, of course, by some accident of inheritance... Should Offa's daughter one day inherit Mercia, for instance, their joint territory would stretch from the Welsh border to the North Sea without a break! It was a startling prospect and the more the fertile mind of the Queen dwelt upon it the more impressive it became. One great kingdom, perhaps, instead of these small rival factions... Yes – it could happen. But not, of course, under such a mild fellow as Ethelbert! He and Alfrida could never administer their rule with sufficient firmness and strength. But Offa – now he was a different prospect. And she, Quendrida, would not be afraid to play her part. Without more ado she took herself into a téte a téte with her husband, pointing out that if the bridegroom died before the ceremony his kingdom might be annexed in one quick stroke and history brought forward!

All unsuspecting, the Princess Alfrida was counting the hours to her bridegroom's arrival at the palace (the site we now know as Sutton Walls in Herefordshire) and King Ethelbert was assembling his entourage ready for the journey westward. Almost from the outset the young king's progress was hindered by a series of strange occurrences. First the earth shook beneath his horse as he attempted to mount; then darkness fell suddenly at noonday. The saintly king bid his party prostrate themselves on the ground whilst he prayed. The chronicler of this tale adds that it was rather a long prayer. It must have seemed so to the prostrated ones – but when darkness lifted, on they all went.

Nearing Offa's kingdom the bridegroom had a mysterious vision. He saw the roof of his own palace sinking and (more disconcerting still) the corners of his bridal bed collapse. Next he glimpsed his mother standing by, weeping blood! Then the situation dramatically changed. He glimpsed a tree – the most beautiful of a group – growing up through the centre of his house and men were chopping at the roots with all their strength so that a torrent of blood flowed forth! But rounding off this startling vision was the sight of a column of light more splendid than the sun, and a wonderful bird with gold tips to his wings soaring upwards into the sublime harmony of heaven. Ethelbert then woke and related it all to his party. It should have made them very thoughtful indeed.

But the trouble with visions is that they may be interpreted in more ways than one and, even though fearful, the courtiers sought to reassure themselves and their king it simply meant that Ethelbert would reach greater power and excellence than any king before him. So – inspired more by his immediate prospects than future ones – the bridegroom pressed on and was presently espied from an upper balcony of her father's palace by his bride-to-be, as he approached with his military train behind him.

Unfortunately he was seen also by another waiting watcher, a servant of King Offa named Winebert, who probably knew the East Anglian king personally; he had been brought up in the household of Ethelbert's father. On receiving his cue he sallied forth from the palace to greet and identify the bridegroom with a kiss of welcome before ushering him ahead of his party inside the big doors. Then, before the rest of the travellers could follow, the doors swung to and they were barred from entering. Their utter consternation can be imagined.

Inside the palace the princess's joyful greeting was cut short at the sight of Winebert advancing menacingly upon her groom. Simultaneously Ethelbert realised his lonely plight and in a matter of seconds grasped the import of all the ominous warnings that had attended his way. For a man of his upbringing and spiritual grasp it may well have been the memory of that 'Judas kiss', even more than the now upraised sword, which signalled his fate. He had come unknowingly as a lamb to the slaughter. He surrendered his soul to God as his body fell decapitated beneath the sword. Immediately the distraught princess flung herself to the ground and acclaimed her stricken groom as 'a martyr whose glorious death made him a sharer of heavenly joys.'

This really was a reprehensible crime, even by the crude standards of that day. The body of the king was taken up and carried out to the banks of the river Lugg at Marden for hasty burial. But the young princess was outraged. Unafraid she denounced her parents, warning her mother of dire consequences to fall upon her a short time hence. Alfrida then pledged herself to remain unwed all her days, to lead the life of a 'solitary' and spend her years in prayerful devotion.

It may have been due to the girl's faithful vigil that King Offa very soon repented of the dreadful deed and took himself off on a pilgrimage to Rome. On his return he made whatever retribution he could, and had Ethelbert's body exhumed from its temporary grave and brought with honour to Hereford Cathedral, where he erected a magnificent tomb.

Soon Ethelbert was acclaimed as the patron saint of Hereford. Stories abound about great lights shining down upon his two resting places and of wells springing up to bear his name both at Marden and Hereford, while reports of miracle cures also persist in county records. What is rather touching is that for 1,200 years Herefordians have supported that repentant king in making amends by continuing to blazon the name in prominent places of the royal guest whose visit there ended so dramatically.

The
Turnpike
Revolt

THE fellow who tried to smuggle a bag of beans through
the toll gate across Weobley Lane in 1840, must have felt
his heart sink into his boots when his bulging pack was
discovered. He was hauled before local magistrates next day
and, as if the fine of £15 were not harsh enough, his horse was
confiscated too.

There would have been a great deal of local sympathy for
him because the turnpike laws were hated and the toll gates
themselves aroused great resentment. Perhaps only those
traversing a familiar road, only to find a newly erected toll
gate thrown across it, can fully savour the anger and frustration the sight aroused. The gates have been described as
'relics of a barbarous age', and looking back through the pages
of history it is obvious that the turnpike tolls were resented as
furiously as was the poll tax by the humble poor and by the
farmers, whose trading was especially affected.

Many Herefordshire towns were encircled with a ring of toll
bars and gates, and routes into the markets were blocked
against non-payers. Threepence was charged for every horse-
drawn wagon, wain or cart; 2d for oxen or cattle carrying
grain, straw, hay or fodder; while the charge for every drove of
calves, hogs, sheep or lambs was 5d per score. Farmers
thought twice about taking their animals or grain to market
and found other means of disposing of them where they could.
Sometimes only a sample of their goods was taken into the

71

market area, the resulting sales being conducted outside the toll gate. As a result a blight fell upon the markets and the pleasant bustle, activity and comradeship formerly enjoyed was sadly reduced. The concession of toll-free entry to churchgoers and to clergy who were conducting funerals or visiting the sick did little to soothe the animosity aroused by the turnpike laws, which were strictly enforced.

Scenes of violence became a common experience. Mobs descended on the gates at nightfall and took great delight in hacking at them with axes and hurling the pieces on to huge bonfires. It became something of a challenge – a national sport, and was romanticised by the adventuring Welsh across the county border who blacked their faces and dressed in women's clothes to make their spirited forays. They became known as Rebecca's Daughters because of the association in the Book of Genesis with the words 'Let thy seed possess the gate of those which hate them', and an element of religious fervour served to justify the risks taken.

Even after an Act of Parliament in 1734 instituted the death penalty for destroyers of turnpikes, the savage orgy of destruction and the feeling that the lawbreaking was justified through the infringement of men's liberty continued unabated, though perhaps with more stealth. There was so much sympathy for the rioters that a well planned intelligence service was given freely by residents in the locality and if the law officers were busy putting down one fire, word was spread that the coast was clear to sweep on and start another.

But of course there were casualties. In September 1735 three men were caught in the act of destroying a toll gate on the fringe of Ledbury and the high spirited adventure turned into tragedy. All were sentenced to die for the escapade. Two of them were brought to the scaffold in the Castle gaol in Worcester while the third achieved the notoriety of being sent to Tyburn for execution as a warning to a wider public than the county of Hereford.

It might be thought that the Tyburn executioner would be skilled at the task but the story goes that he bungled the hanging of the Herefordshire man. Before the poor fellow could be thrust into a hastily dug grave it was noticed that there were faint signs of life! The awful predicament as to what should be done about him was only solved by the victim expiring from exposure in the rainstorm which was beating upon the sobering scene.

It was the passage of time rather than the efforts of the rebels which eventually prevailed. The turnpike gates were finally abandoned amid great rejoicings in 1867.

Pax Cakes
and
Fat Hen

HEREFORDSHIRE, predominantly an agricultural county, abounds in folklore, superstition, old customs and traditions. Many of these reappear in adjoining counties in similar or slightly modified form. But perhaps the nicest of all genuine Herefordshire customs originated in the earnest wish of a Hentland farmer to pour oil on troubled waters way back in the 18th century. It seems that century old feuds had lingered on between local families from the different cultures of Saxon, Norman or Celtic backgrounds. On Palm Sunday he instituted the custom of everyone staying behind after church service to enjoy a repast of small cakes stamped with the slogan 'Peace and Good Neighbourhood'. They were called Pax Cakes and when the custom spread to other villages, hopefully it served to smooth other troubled waters.

Food and drink feature in many old customs. Nothing breaks down reserve more effectively. Even the ancient custom of family reunions on Mothering Sunday included the bringing home of Simnel cakes to their parents by servant girls and apprentices who had been obliged to leave the family circle to follow up some 'living in' occupation.

The ceremony occurs in the middle of Lent and in the early 1900s the Reverend James Davies read a paper to fellow members of the Woolhope Naturalists' Club in which he revealed how warmly he endorsed it. In common with other parish priests he made a point of welcoming families into the church and using appropriate topics on which to exhort them all. Hospitality and reunion were exemplified very clearly in the story of Joseph celebrating the time when he was restored to his family in Egypt and shared with them from his bountiful store. The New Testament lesson brought in the Feeding of the Five Thousand, and the service culminated in a homily on 'Jerusalem ... above ... which is the Mother of us all'. Obviously the parson himself thoroughly enjoyed the family festival as the Father of his flock.

The same reverend gentleman, somewhat ponderously, went on to give his candid opinion of Simnel cakes, 'of which a little goes a long way. The crust can never have been meant to be eaten, inasmuch as it is of the constitution of mortar spiced with more or less saffron and, as it might be surmised, also with mustard!' Could he have been unfortunate in his baker? Nevertheless this good old man commended the custom 'which kept fresh and lively the blessed memories of home and of raising the hearts of the young who have just entered the battle and the turmoil of life.'

Home life seems also to have been the basis of the ringing of the curfew bell. It is said to have been instituted by William the Conqueror, who decreed that eight o'clock was the time to go to bed and to smother or damp down the fires on the household hearth, the French 'couvre-feu' becoming 'curfew'. The sounding of the curfew bell has often been associated with the limitation of liberty, yet there is something rather heartening in the thought of all those neighbours lighting the candles, donning the nightcap, dampening the fire down and settling to slumber at the same time. It may have helped to dispel the lonely darkness and establish a pattern of sleep for all. Certain charitable persons left bequests in their wills to cover payments for a bellringer to perpetuate the custom, which was extended later as a signal to late travellers on the road. Aymestry, for instance, achieved a reputation for its night bell, which became a signal to guide wanderers to the village shelter for a night's hospitality – a charming interpretation of the Curfew Bell.

Of all ancient feast days, Shrove Tuesday is a popular survivor. Originally instituted for the using up of sweet goods in the household and thus to discourage indulgence during Lent, it became popular in the county as a gala day. Various sports were introduced. Price's *Guide* of 1808 claims that Leominster was the instigator of church bell ringing at noon to summon housewives to start frying pancakes. The communal spirit was later extended to introduce a tug-of-war between men of the village, in some cases approved by the Mayor and Corporation, who provided a rope three inches thick and 38 inches long for the purpose. It must have been quite a ceremony when, on the stroke of four in the afternoon, the rope was tossed out of a window in the market place to the two waiting teams below.

Another lively sport for the market place was 'Threshing the Fat Hen', when a hen was fastened onto a man's back, after which he had bells hung around his body. Other players were blindfolded, provided with boughs in their hands, and bidden to chase the man in the middle with his squawking hen. As he dodged around trying to escape blows from the pursuers' boughs, the bells on his body betrayed his position and set up the chase anew. What the poor hen thought of it all defies imagination, but it was at least more merciful than the cockfights which were also instituted on that day in years gone by. Happily the only sport now seems to be the universally popular Pancake Race!

A charming way of celebrating Palm Sunday (some villagers chose Easter Sunday for it) was the decking of all the graves in the churchyard with spring flowers. They called it Flowering Sunday and it was encouraged by the parish priests not only as a mark of respect for – and remembrance of – the dead, but also as a pointer to the triumph and glory of resurrection after death. The use of foliage came into play again on 1st May each year. An old inhabitant of Kington recalled with much affection the decking of all homes with green boughs. On the 29th of that month everyone set to again, this time garlanding their homes with oak boughs and oak apples to celebrate the restoration of the monarchy after England's lamentable Civil War.

Harvest Homes are still enjoyed today but many Christmas customs have died out. Not many are aware that St Thomas's

Day, 21st December, authorised the women (especially older ones) to go 'a-Thomasing', provided with a receptacle into which local farmers and landowners would heap a gift of corn. Christmas itself, of course, is a custom which has prevailed, though in very different mode to the ones of the distant past. Women were forbidden to enter the house on Christmas morning until the threshold had been crossed by a man. There seems no explanation for this other than the rather feeble one offered by the historian Duncumb that 'all thrifty housewives should be at their household affairs!'

The New Year celebration of Burning the Bush prevailed all over the county, simple though it was, and was kept with enthusiasm despite the early rising at five o'clock in the morning. Farmworkers met in one of the fields to tie together straw bundles fixed to a long pole. When the straw was well alight, one man was despatched to run over twelve acres of ground sown with wheat. To the chant (seemingly irrelevant) of 'Old Cider! Old Cider! Brave old Cider!', bystanders awaited the runner's return, then pounced upon him to ascertain that the lighted straw at the end of his pole still burned. If so, it was a good omen for the corn crop, according to popular thought. What happened if the flame was out on return is a matter for conjecture – presumably a swift runner was chosen. A more sophisticated version of the custom was when twelve (some say 13) bundles of straw were laid in a row and fired. Around the largest one the men gathered and drank their master's health in cider before returning home to a feast of caraway seed cake soaked in cider.

Yet another New Year activity (especially remembered in the parish of Dinedor) was the contest for the privilege of drawing the first pail of water from the well. This (however it looked) was called 'the cream of the well'. It was then presented to some respected neighbour or valued citizen – a hefty New Year greeting. Now came the toast:

'Here's to the plough, the fleece and the pail
  May the landlord ever flourish
  And the tenant never fail.'

To round off the merrymaking came a hearty chorus:

'Here's to thee, Benbow, with thy long horn.
May God send thy master a good crop of corn –
Wheat, rye and barley, and all sorts of grain.
If I live to this time twelvemonth may I drink to thee again.'

Wassailing dates back a very long way though not now heard of anywhere. It was a popular cutom calling for dexterity and nimbleness of foot, when a cake was somehow lodged onto a bullock's horn as he stood in his stall. The outcome, or challenge, depended on which way – before or behind him – the animal would toss the cake when he was pricked from behind with a prong! The cake became a trophy for the bailiff if it fell in front of the bull, or for the farm lads if it sailed behind. But it seems that all equally enjoyed the bucket of cider which concluded this tricky manoeuvre with the drinking of the master's health.

A very solemn and touching ceremony (exclusive to the animal kingdom) hinged upon the legend of oxen kneeling on Old Christmas Eve, which was then dated 5th January. The Rev Francis Kilvert, vicar of Bredwardine, appears to have treated with respect a claim by his old parishioner James Meredith that just once in his long lifetime as a shepherd he had glimpsed such a scene. On Christmas Eve (in or about 1878) at twelve o'clock, he saw in a shaft of moonlight the standing oxen sink to their knees and there remain kneeling and moaning, with tears running down their faces. There seems to be no record of anyone else having that privilege who can corroborate the old man's story, but his vicar was genuinely impressed and recorded it in his famous diary.

There are records of many other old customs and traditions in the county libraries. But perhaps the custom of watching the eclipse of the moon only when reflected in water is peculiar because shared between Herefordians and Hindoos. The eastern race are said to hasten down to the nearest river, or even a tank, when the eclipse is expected and to remain in the water until the time has passed. Herefordians, being of a more practical turn of mind, adopted the practice of watching the eclipse reflected in a pail of water.

The
Kidnapped
Heiress

WALTER de Clifford had almost given up hope of fathering an heir to his baronetcy, to Clifford Castle and to the several other estates which he had inherited in 1221, when, after eight years of marriage, his second wife, Margaret, presented him with a baby daughter.

Little Matilda was born about the year 1240 and all of her childhood was spent at the border castle which gave the family their name. Her father was one of the Marcher barons on whom the King of England depended to protect the realm from incursions from their Welsh neighbours.

But it so happened that Walter de Clifford was on good terms with Llewellyn, the Prince of Wales. Margaret, Walter's wife, was Llewellyn's daughter, and the Prince had won respect through his wise and prosperous rule in Wales. Matilda would have learned very early in life that her Welsh ancestry was a more distinguished one than she could claim through the Cliffords. Doubtless she got to know her grandfather quite well. She would have crossed the border to visit him, and from time to time he would have joined the Clifford family in the great hall of the castle where they wined, dined and mingled with their retainers, servants and friends.

A rather curious relationship with the English royal family existed too, a kinship which was to affect Matilda's future very pointedly. That family tie had arisen through the famous romance between Henry II and Rosamund Clifford, the borderland beauty who was to go down in history as Rosa Mundi (Rose of the World) and who bore Henry two illegitimate sons. When Matilda was five or six years old her father received an intimation from the King that a marriage between her and William Longespée (or Longsword), a descendant of Rosamund, would be desirable. It seems likely that the King was desirous of bringing the Clifford estates and the guardian-ship of that important borderland into the ownership and control of Fair Rosamund's descendant – who was also, of course, the King's 'half cousin' and protegee.

Walter's immediate reaction to the proposal is not re-corded. But he was an exceedingly belligerent man when aroused which, it seems, occurred quite often. He was known for his quarrels and lawsuits with the Prior of Little Malvern, the Prior of Wenlock and several others over hunting ground rights. Life at Clifford Castle with a man historians describe as cantankerous and 'peppery' cannot always have been a bed of roses.

When the proposal for Matilda's betrothal to William Longespée arrived, it certainly would not have been politic for her father to demur. However, six years later, when the Damsel of Clifford neared twelve years of age and a formal direction came from the King to contract the marrige, it seems that Walter threw caution to the winds. In January 1250 the King's Messenger arrived at the castle with a royal letter. Whether this was the actual royal command to Walter to forward the marriage project cannot be established for sure, because it disappeared for ever. Walter de Clifford compelled the unfortunte man to eat the entire document, seal and all.

For this 'violent and disgraceful' behaviour, as it is descri-bed in old records, Walter suffered severe penalties at the hands of the King and barely escaped with his life. However, as the time for consummation of the marriage was not far off, and the King's wishes were to be fulfilled, the bride's father had his losses reduced, paid a fine of 1,000 marks and accepted banishment to his estates for the rest of his life. Matilda married William.

But Matilda's story was far from ended. Before the young husband could succeed to his grandfather's title as Earl of

Salisbury, and shortly after a daughter was born, he lost his life in a tournament. The young widow was left again to become sole heiress to the Clifford estates and those of her late husband. In the marriage market she was a rich prize indeed. Henry III began to speculate on the possibility of another match with one of his cousins from across the Channel.

The issue was settled dramatically when Sir John Giffard of Brimpsfield swept down upon the young widow and abducted her! Against her will he carried her off to his own castle and forced her into marriage. How he contrived to detain her there and for how long is uncertain, but eventually the unhappy Matilda managed to get a message to the King – she had been abducted and was being kept against her will by Sir John. The kidnapper was summoned to appear before the King, and declared the charge was false. It was true, he admitted, that he had married Matilda Longespée without the King's permission and he offered the King a fine of 300 marks in retribution. He asserted, however, that he could prove the lady had consented.

The King, it appears, was no Solomon come to judgement. He postponed the issue until 10th March 1270, requesting the lady to appear in person and repeat her complaint. If then she could show that she was 'not content', her husband was ordered to stand trial a month after Easter. Sadly Matilda was reported to be too unwell to attend the hearing. Commissioners were sent to interview her, but somehow the King failed to get a true report. Was Matilda still under duress? Or was the King willing to be satisfied and close the argument because Sir John was a very good supporter of his?

It may be, of course, that Matilda had simply given up the struggle. She already had a daughter by Sir John and was probably pregnant again. A historian records him as 'her vigorously rapist second husband'. So perhaps, in the end, she could not bring to judgement the father of the three daughters she bore him, nor abandon them into his custody. But her complaint ensured that he did not obtain possession of the Clifford estates or those of William Longespée, which passed to the daughter born to him and Matilda before that disastrous tournament. Hopefully she had a more tranquil life than her mother, who endured childhood with a hot-tempered father and more than twelve years of marriage to a man she could never love.

Strangely, the Lady Matilda was to die in the same year in which her Welsh grandfather met a disastrous end. After years of peace, trouble flared up in 1282 between the English King and the Welsh Prince. Llewellyn was cornered on the bridge over the river Irvon by a force led by Sir John Giffard, his granddaughter's brutal husband. The Prince was struck down, beheaded, and his body dragged to a crossroad junction for burial. His head was sent to the King to be crowned in mockery. When the sad report was conveyed to his granddaughter – doubtless by her triumphant husband – her grief must have been great. But hastily she fled to Archbishop Peckham (who had actually been at the scene and witnessed the Prince's death) and implored him to absolve Llewellyn and allow him to be reburied in consecrated ground. Sadly, she was not granted that comfort by His Grace, nor was the great Welsh Prince of whom all Cambria was proud, granted that final dignity.

Was it perhaps of a wounded spirit that Matilda died in the closing days of that tragic year?

Baptism
of Fire

IN the summer of 1899 the son of a Deputy Chief Constable was completing his education at the Lady Hawkins Grammar School in the family's home town of Kington. When most other schoolboys were becoming enamoured with the newly published escapades of *Stalky & Co* and of the wily *Raffles*, young Wilkins Fitzwilliam Chipp was concentrating on real adventure. War clouds were hanging over Britain. The Boers and the British were locked in conflict in South Africa. Ladysmith was under siege. By September the young school leaver had enlisted in the First Herefordshire Rifle Volunteer Corps and begun an involvement with the British Forces which would dominate his life for more than 50 years and take him to many far flung areas of what was then the British Empire. The years were also to earn him a very distinguished record of service to this country.

He later transferred to the Territorial Regiment and the day following the declaration of the First World War saw him mobilised with the rank of Colour Sergeant, embarking for Gallipoli with the First Battalion the Herefordshire Regiment.

When his division reached Suvla Bay, each man was handed two days ration of bully beef and water before being stealthily conveyed by boat, under cover of darkness, to land on the beach of the island of Lemos. At daybreak they took the Turkish army by surprise and (despite heavy shelling from the enemy once they had recovered) drove them resolutely inland to a distance of about three miles.

The British had to fight every dogged inch of the way. Enemy machine guns, as the young Colour Sergeant was to

comment later, were as plentiful on the ground as flowers. The Turkish snipers – men and women – were completely disguised with green paint and their guns so well concealed that it seemed impossible to silence their fire. Both the Colonel and the Adjutant leading the British attack fell among the many casualties, and to Colour Sergeant Chipp fell the responsibility of halting the advance. His immediate problem was to decide where to entrench, take stock of the situation, and endeavour to hold out through the long, cold night which was so great a contrast to the heat endured throughout that exhausting day. It was now some 24 hours since the battalion had left their troopship in Suvla Bay.

Through the hours of darkness the enemy kept up their attack. By morning light the Britishers' water bottles were empty and the bully beef so salty as to be uneatable. Their situation three miles from base, with provisions all gone, provided the NCO with his first real crisis since taking command. Water supplies were vital, but every well was a death trap covered by an enemy machine gun. What it meant to the Colour Sergeant to order six men out to fetch water under unremitting fire is revealed in the letter he later sent to HQ:

'Poor Bill Faulkner was shot through the heart. . . Young Briggs from Presteigne is a real brave kid; he went with six to try and get water. The six were killed and he had three bullets cut his uniform without being wounded and we lost our water bottles. . . At last we got some, and it was one pint between seven men. The same on Wednesday, and on Thursday we had a quarter of a pint each.'

In fact, it was not until late on Thursday night, nearly five days after leaving the troopship, that the division was relieved and the survivors could stumble back the three miles to the beach. At 3 am they received their first rations since the previous Sunday's meagre distribution, and snatched a few hours respite.

On that Friday night the division was thrust into a new attack. They drove the enemy back and held them after capturing a number of German officers along with several hundred Turks. It was no easy task to take the prisoners. They fought off capture with vehemence. But as Sergeant Chipp commented later, 'when you can get near enough they won't stand the bayonet.' (So Corporal Jones of TV's *Dad's Army* was right!). Among the captured green-painted snipers was one woman who had 'acquired' no less than 60 Britishers' identification discs, while a male prisoner had accumulated over £70 in British money.

Just as darkness fell that night Sergeant Chipp received a bullet wound that put him out of action. By daylight he had been brought back to the beach, where he found the field hospital under shell fire. Somehow he got out to the hospital ship for onward transfer to Malta for surgery. It was from the canvas hospital overlooking the Mediterranean Sea that he wrote his account of the Suvla Bay landing and added one further tribute: 'The Ghurkas were on our flank – fine little chaps. . .'

Thus ended the Colour Sergeant's first challenge on active service. It earned him immediate promotion to Company Sergeant Major and by November he had received his commission. In the long wartime struggle that followed, the same resourceful courage and steady nerve which had emerged in the Dardanelles was to be conspicuous in other theatres of war. He served in Mesopotamia and Palestine, winning the Military Cross for distinguished conduct. As Acting Major he later led his battalion to France where Sir Douglas Haig mentioned him in despatches and the French President conferred on him the Croix de Guerre with palms. In operations near Soissons he succeeded Colonel Lawrence as CO and there won the Companionship to the Distinguished Service Order twice over (a bar being added to that decoration). The Belgians also conferred the Croix de Guerre on him and he returned to Britain in 1918 as the most decorated member of the Herefordshire Regiment.

At the investiture at Buckingham Palace in June 1919 the Major received triple honours from King George V and it might have been supposed, in the euphoria of that first year of peace, that his adventures were over. But this was not to be.

He went out to India and Malaya to work in the Forest Service and was soon back in uniform again as an officer in the Malay States Volunteer Regiment. Here a very different challenge awaited him.

In 1939 the Second World War broke out. Major Chipp – now promoted to Lieutenant Colonel and with the OBE added for his services with the Malay Volunteers – was in Singapore on the disastrous day when the Japanese blew up the causeway between the Malayan mainland and the island of Singapore. It was 30th December 1942, and all those on the island were sealed in, waiting only till the island's defendants ran out of ammunition – and hope. That traumatic day came on Black Friday, the 13th of February at 8.30 in the evening. Though some fighters (and possibly Colonel Chipp among them) felt it was too soon to surrender, the die was cast. The stunned inhabitants of Singapore faced the prospect of the kind of inhuman captivity for which the Japanese had become noted – or suicidal attempts at escape.

During the heartbreaking four and a half years that followed Lt Col Chipp shared the horrors and appalling misery of life in Changi Prison Camp in the former British barracks at the east end of Singapore, surrounded by a twelve foot high barbed wire fence. Somehow, though deprived of the right to show any insignia of rank, he and fellow officers were permitted to command their own units, and their proved ability for leadership was concentrated on the attempt to create some sort of order out of a camp which had been built for 1,000 troops and now held 40,000 prisoners. Shacks with bunks were built out of lumber, old rice sacks formed 'mattresses', oil drums made cooking pots, and soup tins became drinking cups. The Malay Volunteers being, so to speak, on home ground had amassed what useful articles they could, together with any tinned provisions still available on the island. It was probably they who acquired the stock of books to form the camp library, and Lt Col Chipp was appointed to be the Changi Librarian. Somehow the officers in Changi preserved some semblance of military life among the vast crowd of captives, and contributed to some kind of sanity through it all. Hopefully Colonel Chipp, in his dealings with fellow sufferers, and despite the terrible contrast to his former life of changing scenes, was able to inspire others with some of his own resourceful spirit.

He survived the captivity which has become notorious for its brutality and returned to England in 1946. By now he was 64 years old, but ten years later he made his last appearance in uniform with the Home Guard which provided the guard of honour in Westminster Abbey at the tomb of the Unknown Warrior. Standing there in the quiet dignity of that beautiful place he must have reflected on his more than 50 years of soldiering since participating in his first guard of honour to King George's father, Edward VII, at the beginning of that king's nine-year reign. He had seen history in the making and had helped in a measure to fashion it. He had seen suffering and sacrifice, the demise of Britain's Empire, and dramatic changes over much of the globe. Colonel Chipp still had 14 years ahead of him and those years in civilian life were enriched by a close association with the Royal Commonwealth Society in London. He was virtually 'a man for all seasons'.

The Legend of Lady Bluefoot

Lady Bluefoot, all in black,
Silver buttons down her back,
Harigoshee! Harigoshee!
Lock the cupboard and take the key!

WHO was she – the poor lady whose sad spirit was supposed to wander around Stapleton Castle in the years following the Civil War? Did she ever exist? Or was she the figment of a storyteller's imagination?

Certainly the people who lived on both sides of the county border in the north-western area of Herefordshire became sufficiently impressed by the tale to be nervous of passing the castle at night even after it had fallen into disuse. It is said that those returning from Presteigne Fair hurried anxiously by, and the rhyme which sprang up naming the mysterious lady as 'Bluefoot' became a familiar chant among children with which to scare each other.

It was actually at an old farmhouse in Presteigne, just inside the adjoining county of Radnorshire, that a faded notebook was discovered containing a handwritten account of the legendary events. It was entrusted to the local historian and writer, the late W. H. Howse to weave it into print in 1946 as part of his book *The History and Legend of Stapleton Castle*. The handwritten manuscript and its phraseology, styled as a melodrama, suggest that it was penned in the early years of the 19th century. It makes fascinating reading.

The story opens with Lady Stapleton as a young widowed mother left with a child after her husband is killed in a stag hunt. The villain of the tale is the steward, Morgan Reece, who misuses his authority when running the estate by victimising workers and tenants alike.

Before young Everard Stapleton became old enough to challenge the evil steward, he was whisked away to boarding school. With no father to guide and influence him, the widowed mother yielded him up with reluctance. But within six months came alarming news. He had disappeared from the school leaving no clue as to how and why. When weeks had elapsed without news of him his distraught mother collapsed. 'Her spirits sank beneath the load of anguish,' says the anonymous author of the manuscript, 'and for many weeks her life was considered doubtful.'

By this time the steward had inveigled himself into his mistress's confidence with a daily audience, rousing her from her weak state with a show of concern for the boy, and pretended efforts to trace him. Then occurred a dramatic change in what turned out to be the steward's final interview with his lady. Domestic staff were astonished to see 'her pale cheeks glowing with passion and her mild eyes burning with resentment.' Her ladyship would not divulge the reason to her servants but informed them 'Ere three days are passed the discovered fiend shall pollute my roof no more.' During the night that followed, the lady's maid was aroused by the sound of a shriek. She broke out of sleep and listened. All seemed quiet, however, and she resumed her slumbers.

But when morning came, the customary summons from Lady Stapleton was so long delayed that the maid tapped apprehensively on her mistress's door. No answer came to repeated taps and calls, so the now frightened girl summoned other servants. Entering together they were all horrified to find their mistress's lifeless form lying against her couch; a large hunting knife that had been her husband's lay at her side, and a pool of blood stained the carpet. A long gash in the lady's throat had obviously ended her life. The scene suggested suicide.

Morgan Reece testified that the reason for the lady's agitation, witnessed by the servants, had been a proposal of marriage from him which the lady had scornfully rejected. He admitted also that she accused him of the abduction of her son. But his demeanour and protestations seemed to indicate innocence in any involvement in her death. No further evidence was forthcoming and the poor lady was taken for burial, probably in unconsecrated ground. That alone, coupled with the servants' unease and the maid's tale of the shriek in the night, was enough to set tongues wagging and to start off speculation that the poor lady had been doubly wronged – in death and in burial – and would not rest in peace.

Apparently there was no peace for those remaining in the castle. Morgan Reece took himself off to join Cromwell's army. One by one the domestics left, convinced they saw and heard unnatural occurrences – a moving form, unexplained lights in unoccupied rooms, and sometimes the echo of a midnight cry . . . all the ingredients of a good mystery and a haunting legend.

Most legends end on a sombre note, but the handwritten manuscript so well presented by Mr Howse (who then lived in Presteigne) should have gone a long way to dispel fears and reassure nervous travellers on the road which passes the castle, for eventually truth and justice prevailed.

Everard Stapleton returned to the castle, ten years after his disappearance and with a tale of astonishing adventures. Beginning with his abduction from school by an agent of Morgan Reece, he had been lured on to a sea-going vessel, shipwrecked in the Atlantic, and rescued into the care of a Puritan voyager who was on his way to a new life in America. Here the boy lived beneath this good man's roof and in due time won the heart of a demure and beautiful maiden, Mercy. Together they unravelled the mysteries of what happened on that last day of Lady Stapleton's life and during the tragic night. Evidence of Reece's guilt of his mistress's murder came to light in a locked cupboard. A struggle between

Everard and Reece (who had rushed to the castle on hearing of Everard's unexpected return) brought about the latter's death, and the tale of his guilt followed him to the grave.

It is true, of course, that the unfortunate Lady Stapleton could not be restored to life. But her remains were moved to an honoured place in a vault below Prestiegne church, a mile from the castle itself. This accomplished, the young couple bid a final farewell to Everard's childhood home and set off to begin a new life.

Thus justice was done, the truth revealed, Everard was comforted and the people who live on each side of the county border may rest assured that 'Lady Bluefoot' has been avenged. The cabinet which contained the incriminating evidence had yielded up its secrets. Nothing remained but to 'lock the cupboard and take the key.'

A Storm
in a
Pewter Pot

'Johnny's so long at the fair –
He promised to buy me a bunch of blue ribbon
To tie up my bonny brown hair...'

THAT popular little ditty conjures up a pleasing picture of old time rural simplicity – and of low expectations in the field of luxuries! The girl who waited so trustingly for her 'fairing' would have envied her Johnny his day out.

In Herefordshire at least 15 annual fairs flourished in the villages. Sadly those along the border with Wales had to forego all the activity and excitement of a fair day because of danger from Welsh raiding parties. On a September day in the year 1400, after a truce of some years duration, Owen Glendower had suddenly risen like a giant awakened and descended in fury upon a market fair in the Marcher plain below. Stallkeepers, traders, entertainers and customers must have been petrified when the sudden swift charge of yelling horsemen and blaring war horns broke in upon their festive scene, thundered along the length of the merchants' stalls and destroyed anything and everything within reach. Merchant stallholders, tenants of the English Marcher Lord Grey who had incensed the Welsh leader, tried in vain to protect their booths and themselves. In the space of a few terrifying moments the happy village scene was changed to one of carnage and devastation.

After this all Herefordshire fairs took place well inside the county border and usually in villages equidistant from the main towns and cities. For many years annual Saints Day fairs were conducted at Much Marcle, Hampton Bishop, Much Cowarne, Kilpeck, Thruxton, Madley, Preston, Moccas, Staunton, Kinnersley, Winforton, Pembridge, Wigmore, Kington and Brampton Bryan with great success. Apart from the practical business of the day, excitement and novelty was generated by the influx of traders, entertainers, sideshows, barrel organs, and quack doctors or chemists hoarsely proclaiming their magic cures. The chance to see new faces from the world outside was added to the pleasure of renewing acquaintances, indulging in a little horseplay with other lads, and perhaps a spell in the boxing ring.

However, the fair was important, too, because decisions might be made there which would shape the course of a man or woman's life for at least the year ahead. It was an opportunity for hiring labour, and those seeking work customarily brought and displayed the tools of trade which would indicate their skills to any prospective employer – a shepherd's crook, a milking stool or a waggoner's whip served as a badge of office . . . or of servitude, for over many generations the lot of farm workers was not to be envied. A contract made between farmer and workman at a hiring fair, even if by word of mouth alone, was recognised as binding. A defaulter was subject to fines, imprisonment or even a physical beating! Moreover, a married man would be expected to commit the services of wife and family in addition to his own, in return for meagre accommodation.

In the towns and cities, of course, a much bigger fair could be staged, but only if granted by charter from the king. Great financial advantages and privileges came with the charter. The one awarded to the Bishops of Hereford granted a three days' fair in the time of King Henry I, but this was later extended to nine days and was a very highly organised affair indeed. The market area in Hereford extended from St Peter's church in the east of the city, to All Saints' church in the west. It contained a Butcher's Row, a Customs House and a preaching cross alongside its market stalls and booths.

The Bishop was granted a wide range of civil powers for the period of the fair. The government of the city was transferred from the Mayor and Corporation and handed over to the Bishop, lock, stock and barrel, in a ceremony when the keys of the city were placed into his hands. He then held complete jurisdiction over the citizens, was empowered to sit in judgement (in person or through his steward) in the courts, and to pass sentence upon offenders as he saw fit. In addition he was entitled to extract a toll from every trader. Even when citizens successfully petitioned to be allowed to sell goods from their own houses during the fair period, they had to agree to pay the Bishop's toll. This led to some very strained relations between Church and citizens on occasions, as happened on the eve of the fair celebrating the Feast of St Dennis in Hereford in the October of 1520.

A Sergeant of the King's Mace, one William Hill, was authorised to distrain a carpet and pewter pot from a woman named Ann Gough, presumably in default of a fine. Having secured the goods he set out to deliver them to a pound where the civil authorities normally stored such articles before selling them to recover the debt. However, he rather unwisely took a short cut through the cathedral grounds and had the misfortune to be challenged about the business by Nicholas Walwyn, who is described in an old report as being 'one of the residentiaries of the Cathedral Church'. Though the fair had not yet begun (presumably this was the evening before) the said Nicholas Walwyn took it upon himself to claim the goods on behalf of the Bishop, giving as his authority the civil powers with which the prelate was invested during the fair.

The report, in the rather quaint language of the day, then highlights the argument which followed the bailiff's refusal. The Bishop's man

> 'pulled the sergeant by the head and would have taken the distraint from him. Notwithstanding the sergeant brought the distress to Richard Phillips, then Mayor of the City, and showed him how he was dealt with. Whereupon the Mayor, his brethren, and the whole commonalty were sore grieved.'

However Walwyn was not prepared to give up without a struggle. He organised a group of church dignitaries, including two archdeacons, nine chapter members, their steward and some others, who took themselves to the Mayor and asked for the case to be investigated. To this the Mayor agreed and by mutual consent three Church arbitrators were appointed to meet the Town Clerk and two of 'the Mayor's brethren' at eight o'clock in the morning in the Chapter House. So while, presumably, the fair got under way for those engaged in less serious matters, the six arbitrators met and eventually pronounced judgement – that the belligerent Nicholas Walwyn (the Bishop's champion) should pay the offended sergeant compensation for 'pulling his head'', in the sum of six shillings and eight pence. . .

'and also that the Mayor and Nicholas Walwyn with one Mr Brayne, another of the residentiaries who, as the Mayor was informed, did provoke the said Walwyn to take the distress from the sergeant, should appear in the Cathedral Church at two o'clock in the afternoon on the Feast of St Luke, there to meet and take each other by the hands, and for a sign and token of love between the Church and City should go from thence to one William ap Thomas Goldsmith's tavern. At which hour they appeared in the said church and there Nicholas Walwyn paid six shillings and eight pence, of which sum, for further amity and love, the Mayor willed the sergeant to omit five shillings; at whose desire he was content. Thereupon, as lovers and friends, they went arm-in-arm to the tavern and the Canons of the Chapter there gave wine to the Mayor and others to the value of twenty pence. And the Mayor delivered the distress to one Ann Gough and took no more for fine therof but two pence for a quart of wine.'

And all for the sake of a carpet and a pewter pot!

The Hound
of
Hergest

IN Kington church, lying tranquilly side by side in the cool
dimness, are the effigies of a man and his wife of the 15th
century. There is little to show that here lie Ellen the Terrible
and 'Black' Vaughan!

Ellen Gethin, as she was before her marriage, lived in that
turbulent time when the Wars of the Roses flared up again
and again. Life must have seemed cheap at the time and many
a man was guilty of taking life, yet Ellen Gethin, for one act of
revenge, has gone down into history branded with the title
'Ellen the Terrible'. Is murder more reprehensible when
committed by a woman?

In Ellen's case the man she killed had slain her brother and
had not been brought to book. When she knew he would be
competing in an archery tournament, she herself practised in
deadly earnest and entered the field on the tournament day
dressed as a man. Manoeuvring herself into a favourable
position she raised her bow and in cold blood shot an arrow
into the heart of John Vaughan, killing him instantly. Somehow in the resulting confusion she made her escape, swiftly
divesting herself of her tournament gear.

Ellen apparently got away with the murder. The victim was
a member of a prominent Herefordshire family, who made an
impact on the county's history through several generations. It
seems quite remarkable that this premeditated murder, cast-
ing such a blight on the lively anticipation and excitement of

the tournament, escaped retribution from such a powerful and influential family as the Vaughans, to whom Ellen Gethin herself was related. John Vaughan was her cousin.

Even more remarkable, then, was her marriage at a later date to another Vaughan cousin. He had been christened Thomas but is referred to in all the county records as 'black' Vaughan, a name usually attributed to the colour of his hair – in contrast to a red-haired brother known as 'Red' Vaughan. If he knew of his wife's exploit then he was a plucky man, or perhaps he admired her loyalty. It seems that the couple lived together in harmony at Hergest Court near Kington.

Poor Thomas met his violent death in 1469 when called upon to defend his king, Edward IV, after a Lancastrian rebellion flared up in Warwickshire. He had the misfortune to be captured by the rebels in the battle of Banbury and was summarily beheaded before the Yorkist forces could rescue him. Since he was defending a reigning monarch it seems rather hard that he should have suffered the death normally reserved for traitors and rebels.

But the legend that has pursued Thomas Vaughan down the years is anything but tranquil. Though little has been discovered that was detrimental to him in his lifetime (only one writer vaguely refers to him as a tyrant) it is said that his restless spirit returned to haunt his home at Hergest Court, and that subsequently it took twelve parsons to exorcise his ghost! The twelfth (and successful) exorcist is supposed to have cast the ghost into a snuff box and flung it into Hergest Pool.

All who were involved in this strange adventure must have retired in satisfaction, for peace was then restored to the Court. But what makes Black Vaughan's story unusual – if not unique – is the sequel, which says that a hundred years later some unsuspecting diver retrieved the snuff box and released the ghost! From then on it took a new form – possibly as a result of Thomas's name of 'Black' Vaughan – and roamed the grounds and pool-side of Hergest as a big black dog. Its only function, apparently, was to howl as a warning of imminent death in the Vaughan family.

All in all it is a strange tale, but it seems that it caught the imagination of Sir Arthur Conan Doyle when he visited relatives in the district and formed the basis for his famous story *The Hound of the Baskervilles*. The author's skilful pen wove the plot so convincingly that it has somehow added credence to the Hergest legend. And what a comfort it is to have the adroit mind of Sherlock Holmes to throw light upon that haunting mystery!

Prince Edward's Flight

IT was a bitter pill Prince Edward had to swallow when, on 14th May 1264, he surrendered his sword to his uncle, Simon de Montfort. Years of bickering between Edward's father, King Henry III, and the English Parliament had finally flared into open conflict, in what has become known as the Barons' War. What made it so galling for Prince Edward was that he himself had fought magnificently and thought the battle won, only to return from his own successful foray to find the King in the custody of his sister's husband, Earl Simon de Montfort who demanded the prince's surrender as a hostage.

The 19 year old prince, whose splendid physique and height had earned him the nickname Longshanks, had many faults. He was at times imperious and overbearing. To submit to the messenger who brought his uncle's demand was the hardest thing he had ever done but it eased his father's plight.

As soon as the King's captors subdued the city of Hereford, their royal prisoner was brought to lodge in the castle there. Meanwhile Prince Edward languished in several different prisons until he too was brought to Hereford Castle and placed in the custody of his cousin Hal, Earl Simon's eldest son. Hal – the Lord Henry de Montfort – was only about one year older than Prince Edward, but had always been of a sober and responsible nature. He had gained a reputation for honesty and sincerity and looked for the same qualities in others. He did not relish the situation which now gave him authority over the cousin who, even in boyhood, had demanded recognition as the future King of England. Nevertheless Hal shared his father's passionate desire to see the country ruled justly and wisely and made no bones about sharing those aspirations with the captive Prince.

After a year in captivity there came a day when, looking out over the grounds of the castle from a lookout on its summit, the Prince spoke to Hal of his frustration at being denied the freedom of the open fields where they had cantered so often in happier times. The cousins were, of course, experienced horsemen. The Prince had not been in the saddle for more than a year. Now it was mid-summer and he expressed a longing to feel the rush of wind through his hair and the exhilaration of speeding over the familiar turf. Torn between his natural sympathy and his sense of responsibility, Hal searched his conscience. Was it possible, under strict surveillance, to allow the Prince such a canter? Hal had at least four local lords, expert horsemen, on whom he could call to share the guardianship for an hour or so. He had but to send a message to each of them at Lyonshall, Ewyas Harold, Snodhill and Much Marcle, and they would immediately respond. The more he thought about it, the more convinced Hal became that no harm could come of such a project, and it might do the Prince a power of good. Surely Edward would not take advantage, even if he could? Hal would extract his promise on that score.

But Hal was a wishful thinker. He should have known that keeping his word was not Prince Edward's strong point. In certain circumstances the Prince felt perfectly justified in breaking an oath. As soon as his cousin broke the welcome news that an hour on Tillington Common was to be arranged on the following day, the Prince's fertile mind got to work. Tillington was five miles away and was on the direct road north to Wigmore Castle, home of the Mortimers who were loyal to the King! The Prince had for some time been allowed the services of his personal servant, and the man slipped away overnight to acquaint the Mortimers with the news.

After despatching his messenger to Wigmore Castle the Prince gave the matter even greater thought. What mount might be given to him he could not know. That there could be half a dozen armed horsemen alongside him in the field was a challenge. Could he expect to outrun them all, even given the advantage of surprise? Somehow he must devise a scheme to tire their mounts without doing so to his own. There must be a way!

On Tillington Common the following day the Prince shot an eager glance around him. His gaze did not linger long on the beauties of the Black Mountains and Brecon Beacon to the west, or on the gentle, undulating hills surrounding the common. The wooded hill of Badinage immediately to the north was the focus of his quick scrutiny. The Prince's own squire had been allowed on this expedition, and while his master began to skirmish boisterously around the common, the squire picked his way slowly and thoughtfully toward the northern fringe.

Soon Prince Edward was in festive spirits and, exerting all his charm, he begged his unsuspecting cousin Hal to let him try his mount. He then careered at high speed around the open field before returning Hal's horse, now sweating and tired with the exertion. As if to compliment the four local lords on their splendid mounts the Prince went to each in turn, and incredibly they all responded to the laughing captive and allowed him to skirmish around the field on each horse in turn, working off his own energy – and that of the spirited animals he rode! It would have been difficult not to admire such a man who could come out of a year's confinement and give such a spirited exhibition.

When the agreed time was up and Hal summoned the party to return to Hereford, the Prince mounted his own horse which had been standing by, cropping a clump of grass here and there. He made to turn toward Hereford with the party and then suddenly made a lightning dash toward his own squire, who was pacing the northern boundary of the common. 'After him', yelled Hal de Montfort, and swung his mount in pursuit. The others followed, urging their beasts forward with all possible speed – only to realise with shock and anger that the horses were too tired to maintain the speed of the fleeing Prince. His horse, of course, had reserved its strength during the past hour. Now it did not fail the Prince, who skirted the ridge around the common and reached a point where the standard of the Mortimers was clearly visible –

borne aloft by a group of armed horsemen awaiting the Prince with huge delight.

By now the pursuers realised their task was hopeless. Filled with chagrin and dismay, Henry de Montfort led his party back to Hereford. What would be the consequences of his rash misjudgement of the Prince's willpower and capabilities? Not all of England was on the side of the barons and de Montfort. Could Edward raise a force which would now challenge Parliament? If so, Hal was justified in the fearful foreboding which now clutched his heart.

Sadly for the de Montforts and their allies those worst forebodings were realised. After jubilantly conducting Prince Edward to sanctuary in Wigmore Castle, 20 miles north of Hereford, Roger Mortimer and his neighbouring Marcher barons joined the Prince in an army which was to restore power to the King and bring death and destruction to the Prince's uncle and his cousin, Hal. Earl Simon suffered the indignity of a traitor's death, though, mercifully, it was on the battle field, where his body was hacked about and his head struck off. It was Roger Mortimer who, exultant with triumph, perpetrated this deed and actually despatched the Earl's head to Lady Mortimer, his own wife at Wigmore Castle! Only slightly less macabre was the sending of a foot to Prince Llywelyn of Wales, who had been on his way to support Simon – and of a hand to Simon's shocked widow, the Lady Eleanor de Montfort.

It seems that Hal was borne away from the field with greater restraint, possibly under the jurisdiction of the Prince. King Henry, restored to power after being rescued by his son, was not so charitable. He fined the unfortunate citizens of Hereford because of his imprisonment there – an annual sum over the next 14 years.

When the Prince finally came to power as King Edward I, he made a splendid king. It seems that the year of captivity, the hard lessons learned in Hereford Castle and, quite possibly, the integrity of Cousin Hal, were not lost on Edward Longshanks.

A
Fatal Slip
of the Tongue

Two powerful families were united when William de
Braose, the Lord of Bramber, married the neighbouring
heiress, Lady Maud of Hay in the early 13th century. The de
Braoses had their own chief seat in Kingsland, but Lady
Maud brought her husband no less than four other castles
along the Herefordshire/Welsh border – Hay, Radnor, Brecon
and Bredwardine. Fortunately the new Lady of Bramber
brought also a very capable pair of hands and a shrewd brain
with which to adminster the joint estates, because her husband's absences from the country were frequent and often
prolonged. He was a close companion of King John and spent
most of his time in the shadow of that unpopular sovereign.

Lady Maud made a striking impression with her powerful
physique, handsome appearance and seemingly unbounded
energy. In the event of any threat of attack she was fully
capable of defending her properties and had been known to
lead an army into battle – even keeping her own suit of
armour on hand! No captive ever found mercy at her hands.
But she was also a good mother. She brought up her family
with the same firm resolve as she dealt with other duties. In
the course of time beneficial marriages were negotiated for
them, during those interludes when her husband and the King
were sitting round the festal board at one or other of the
family's dining halls. The eldest son married into the House of
Gloucester, which gave him some claim to kinship with King

John, and the daughter became the Baroness de Lacy, which secured some possessions in Ireland.

Maud de Braose found plenty to occupy her energies during her husband's absences. She was quick to recognise potential in the lush pasture lands of Herefordshire and was one of the early cattle breeders in the county. Her speciality was a splendid breed of pure white beasts with just their ears tinged with reddish brown.

To watching neighbours it must have seemed that everything the de Braoses touched turned to gold. But could it last? How much of their good fortune was dependant on their relationship with the King? He was known to be a capricious character whose favour could turn turtle at the slightest provocation. After de Braose had enjoyed the King's confidence for ten years many of the noble families around him began to ask questions. Had the de Braoses some secret hold over the King?

As the King's popularity plunged ever lower in the latter years of his reign, questions were also being asked behind closed doors concerning the great mystery of the day. What had happened to the King's nephew, Prince Arthur? The young Prince of Brittany had been a thorn in his uncle's side for years. He had a very reasonable claim to the English throne despite having spent all his life in Brittany. But John had eventually captured Prince Arthur and imprisoned him. Ugly rumours reached England. Had he indeed ordered a gaoler to blind the Prince? After the Prince was moved to Rouen, what had happened to him? Now there was an ominous silence, following a sinister tale about a rowing boat seen pushing out into the Seine from the castle steps at Rouen. Three figures were glimpsed, one of them said to be bound and weighted... one was thought to be the King – and the other? Who could it have been, men asked, but the custodian of Rouen at that time – William de Braose himself. And was Prince Arthur the one who did not return?

But the questions were not answered. Complete silence greeted all probes, even at Rouen. Only two people could know the truth, the King and the youth's custodian, and maybe the Lady Maud. Was this the secret pact between the

King and his confidant which made the de Braoses so sure of themselves and the security of their position?

If so, it must have come as a shock to the Lord of Bramber one day to be told by the King that he was short of money and needed to sell some land for 5,000 marks – and that he, de Braose, was expected to buy it!

The de Braoses were not in the market for purchasing land. Five thousand marks was a considerable sum for land they did not want – and which, moreover, on investigation did not seem to belong to the King! Two churchmen produced ownership documents and refused to yield them. De Braose went back to the King, stalling for time. But John was not interested in legal niceties. He wanted the money and it was up to de Braose to find it and pursue the problem with the churchmen afterwards! Supported by his wife, the Lord of Bramber held out longer. Had he known all that was to follow he would have swiftly capitulated.

One of the privileges enjoyed by the de Braoses until this point had been exemption from the custom of the day whereby all noble families sent one child into the service of the Palace – in effect as a hostage against that family's conduct. While the de Braoses were stalling about the land purchase there came a knock on their castle doors. A group of the King's officers stood there and presented an order from the King that a child of the household was to be sent forthwith to become a page to the Queen of England! In that moment the couple knew that their day of favour was over.

Lady Maud reeled back and for one dreadful second she lost her head. Within sound of the party at the doors she vowed, 'I will not deliver any child of mind to a King who murdered his own nephew!' It was the trump card that would have been better if it had never been played. All England might suspect the king, in secret, but this was the wife of the custodian of Rouen citadel who spoke!

Panic set in within seconds. Lady Maud immediately sought to placate the King. Four hundred of her beautiful white cattle were rounded up and sent to the Queen. But to no avail. The cattle became the first item of an inexorable toll that was to lead to the fall of the House of Bramber.

The worst of King John's nature (and it had sordid depths) came into play. He sent messengers to seize the Castle of Bramber – and they found an empty shell. The family had fled with their possessions. Then the King himself led a force to take possession of all the castles brought to the family in the dower of the Lady Maud. In agony of mind, de Braose realised the futility of fighting. He begged audience with the King and pleaded for terms, agreeing instantly to the demand that he pay in full for the land purchase and forfeit the castles of Hay, Brecon and Radnor. Having got out of the King's presence and breathed fresh air again, a disastrous courage returned to de Braose and on impulse he set fire to some property of John's and fled to Ireland with his family.

Later some kind of sanity returned and he ventured to contact the King: This time the price of the land rose to 40,000 marks! It was practically the price of a king's ransom – certainly beyond the means of a private citizen. Negotiations were finally at an end and the family became hunted quarry. Sadly for the Lady Maud, she and her eldest son were captured on the Irish coast and taken to the King at Windsor.

The end of her story is a terrible one. John was merciless. She and her son were walled up alive in a cell in the keep at Windsor Castle. It was not the first time John had killed his victims by starvation. But by any standards whatever, it was a barbarous act perpetrated on the wife of his closest ally and one who had been his hostess so often in the past.

Meanwhile William de Braose escaped to France while John was burning down Hay and Radnor castles. In the year or so of life that remained to the Lord of Bramber, he had time to contemplate not only the wrongs against him but also perhaps to realise that no one in England would regret the fall of the House of Bramber. The de Braoses had made many enemies. The town of Leominster, for example, would certainly not lament their fate, for the townsfolk claim it was at his wife's instigation that de Braose burned down their town.

It is tantalising to read that de Braose actually wrote out a report in France telling the truth about Prince Arthur's fate. But if so, the report never saw the light of day and the Lord of Bramber died in bitterness of soul without having placed his fatal trump card on the table for the world to see.

The Tomkyns Pedigree

ALL over the world, red and white Hereford cattle are recognised as the cream of pedigree breeds, and they have brought lasting fame to the county. The family responsible more than any other for their development were the Tomkyns, who had a respectable pedigree of their own.

The first known Tomkyns appears to have been a wool exporter in 1433; of yeoman stock, he soon became known officially as 'a gentleman of Herefordshire'. For the next 200 years the Tomkyns family enjoyed growing prosperity in Weobley as it developed into a thriving little market town. They began to acquire property, and with the purchase of Garnston from the Earl of Essex came 'lord of the manor' status. Fortunes increased further when the heir became High Sheriff, and it was James Tomkyns who became Deputy Lieutenant in 1618 and the family's first Member of Parliament. Subsequently he was joined by his sons, William and Thomas.

It so happened that the two brothers did not sit in Parliament alongside their father until the spring of 1640, when they found themselves embroiled in the most dramatic scenes in Parliamentary history. The Tomkyns family were among the moderates who viewed the truculence of Puritan Parliamentary extremists with anxiety. About this time James Tomkyns resigned his seat to take an appointment in the King's Household. His elder son died after only a year as MP and Thomas

alone was left to witness the dramatic scenes which unfolded.

It must finally have become obvious to all that Civil War was inevitable. The Queen went to Holland to buy arms, after requesting James Tomkyns, as a member of the royal staff, to raise a troop of cavalry in the City. He had scarcely begun before King Charles left the capital and Parliamentary forces took control there. James was arrested, brought before a military tribunal and sentenced to hang as a traitor to the State. The sentence was carried out in public, before his own office in Fetter Lane! The feelings of his family at Weobley can be imagined.

That scene, whether Thomas witnessed it or not, must have been the son's most painful memory during his later prison solitude. He himself was not arrested until 1643, at a time when it seemed Charles was defeated. He does not appear to have taken part in the war on one side or the other. But when the King had fled the country, Parliamentary rule was unchallenged and the inevitable recriminations began. Informers and opportunists all over the country (there were a couple in Weobley) took pleasure in 'denouncing' royalist sympathisers. The slightest unguarded word or sympathetic look could bring the knock at the door. Tom was arrested, fined over £2,000, deprived of his estates and thrown into the common prison. His wife and ten year old child were left at the mercy of relatives. Fortunately Tom's sister was married to Roger Vaughan of Moccas Court. His was a powerful and influential family, though he could do nothing to help Tom himself. Under Parliamentarian rule Weobley, like everywhere else, had to toe a very strict line. Not until the Restoration was Tom reinstated, granted a pension and became the first Tomkyns to be knighted.

The pension was none too generous but it enabled him to live quietly in the lovely Herefordshire countryside, at peace with his neighbours. This was probably all he asked as he busied himself rebuilding the old family property of Garnston and tending the estate. He enjoyed another 13 years of life in the rich pastureland which, within 20 years, would contribute to the Tomkyns' fortunes.

Enterprise and prestige now swung in a new direction

111

which was to enhance the family name, benefit their county and make an impact around the world. By the year 1700 Richard Tomkyns of King's Pyon was building up an impressive reputation as a breeder of some of the finest cattle to be seen anywhere.

Richard died in 1723 and in a will which has since become famous because of its far reaching consequences, he bequeathed his cattle, naming the animals individually, to each of his six sons. To the fourth son, Benjamin, he left 'the cow *Silver* and her calf'.

As Benjamin was only six years old at the time, it was 15 years before he got his own farm at Court House, Canon Pyon. His farming career of more than 50 years furthered the breeding programme and, joined in time by his son Benjamin the Younger, he had the immense satisfaction of knowing that the future of a very special herd was in good hands. Both Benjamins enjoyed the friendship and professional co-operation of other Herefordshire breeders and developed variation in colour and markings which featured impressively at County agricultural shows.

After all their trials, finally it was the animal with the red body and white face which achieved lasting fame as the Hereford. By 1817 a thriving export trade was underway and soon Herefords were crossing Canada, the United States and Mexico, into the great beef raising areas of South America. More than 50 countries have imported the Herefords because the breed is so hardy as to thrive under almost any conditions in the world, from the prairies to the Russian steppes. In Hereford itself the livestock market held nine times a year keeps alive local awareness of this great asset to the county.

It has been truly said that when Benjamin Tomkins (the name has been slightly modernised) received his splendid inheritance of *Silver*, she was also a legacy to the cattle raising industry of the world.

A
Cider
Miscellany

HEREFORDSHIRE farmers may not have been the pioneers in cider production, but by 1397 the county seems to have outstripped all others for the abundance and popularity of its brew. Consequently stories and anecdotes abound all over the county which feature it.

Most dictionaries give the meaning of the word 'cider' as 'a fermented slightly alcoholic drink prepared from the juice of apples'; yet the old Wycliffe Bible in Hereford Cathedral's famous Chained Library uses the word as a substitute for the more familiar phrase 'strong drink' which appears in most versions of the Bible today. In the first chapter of St Luke's Gospel, concerning the upbringing of John the Baptist, where most of us read 'he shall drink neither wine nor strong drink', the Wycliffe version at Hereford has it: 'he schal not drinke wyn ne sider.' Scholars argue that Herefordians have only a weak case for associating the translation with their popular brew, but that Bible has established itself sufficiently in the world's best chained library to be known as the Cider Bible. Hereford is proud of it, and it is not the only ecclesiastical connection with cider.

Back in the 14th century so prolific was the crop that farmers were paying their church tithes with so many hogs-heads of the brew. It then became so abundant in and around the church that infants were baptised with it. Presumably this ceremony only involved sprinkling on the forehead, so one wonders why it was deemed necessary to pass a law forbidding the use of cider in the baptismal font? Was it for the child's protection or for the infant's sponsors? Whatever the answer, to have to legislate against the custom indicates that it was not abandoned voluntarily.

So what did the parson do with his surplus cider? Fortunately the brew became an accepted form of currency and could be bartered for other goods or services. It was common practice to pay a farm labourer's wages partly in cider. The good health of the county workmen, and their longevity, was attributed by many to the generous drafts which punctuated their working day. During the long hours of harvesting a man would consume as much as three gallons a day without apparent harm. The curious custom of all drinking from the same vessel in the field must have made it something of a ritual, each having to await his turn while the youngest lad ladled out the tots. Perhaps this inconvenience was compensated by a sense of comradeship in the shared cup. Or, maybe, pleasure was increased by anticipation during the waiting and watching.

The workers' cider would undoubtedly be a weak strain made from any and every apple that came to hand. Credit for developing and refining the brew is widely recognised as being due to the first Viscount Scudamore in or around 1630. His orchard of Red Streak Pippins formed the basis, and under his careful husbandry cider became a drink which graced the tables of the well-to-do and rapidly gained favour during times of conflict on the Continent when wine imports almost dried up. It is doubtful whether the workers in these distinguished households got the benefit of the best quality cider as it had to be provided in quite large quantities. The vicar of Dilwyn in the second half of the 1700s fully approved the routine by which 'The ordinary course among their servants is to breakfast and sup with toast and cyder through the whole of Lent, and the same diet continues in the neighbourhood on fasting days all the year round, which lightens their appetite and creates in them durable strength to labour.' It sounds rather feudal, and doubtless the workers had little time for leisure and pleasure, but if any summoned strength to visit the village inn of an evening they might well have enjoyed the fun of watching a stranger or newcomer supping his cider from a 'frog mug'. Affixed to the inside base of the mug was a green china frog poised as if to leap upwards – and only visible to the eye of the startled drinker when he was taking the last gulp.

So cider became universally popular, it seems. John Kyrle, who was High Sheriff of the county in 1683, settled in Ross on Wye and was a marvellous 'all rounder'. Affable in company of his own class and consistently generous to those poorer, he was a do-gooder who was 'nice with it'. He remained a bachelor but loved company and kept open house. Thomas Hearne writes of him: 'He would tell people when they dined or supped with him that he would, if they pleased, let them have wine but that his own drink was cyder, and that he found it most agreeable, and that he did not care to be extravagant with his small fortune. . .' From a man so practical and so well liked this was high praise.

But it is true, of course, that one can have too much of a good thing. The old tale of Adam and Biddy, cottagers in the county, is a case in point. Adam liked his cider rather too well and would roll home drunk. Divorce was then not so easy to come by, so Biddy made an attempt to cure her erring spouse. Dressed from head to toe in a white sheet, she sallied forth one dark night to stand beneath a nearby oak tree and await Adam's homecoming. Bye and bye he came staggering along. Biddy stepped smartly out into his path but made no sound.

'Oo be you then?' queried the swaying husband.
'I be Old Nick' droned Biddy in as deep as voice as she could muster.
'Oh. . . ah. . . Come on in then' responded Adam affably, 'We got one o' your sort inside already!'

It must have been more convenient to drink on your own premises. Lots of smallholders brewed their own cider and in his splendid book *The Leon Valley*, Norman C. Reeves tells a good tale in just such a setting. He got it from a parson, the Reverend George Jobling, and it refers to the potency of the 'residue' left behind after the cider fruit has been crushed and the juice filtered through layers of thick blanket cloth. Thus the solid matter, pips, skin, core, etc, was held back and later thrown out. It soon fermented. It was not unusual for foraging pigs to feed upon it, and probably did the resulting pork no harm as apple sauce is its normal garnish. But on one occasion a few ducks at Cobnash joyfully chanced upon this 'must', as the stuff was known. But it was wintertime, and presently, overcome by a pleasant drowsiness, they rolled over and fell asleep, one by one, and lay on the frozen snow. Hypothermia set in of course, as they were not discovered for some hours. Their owner found the lifeless forms, frozen stiff, but as they had been intended for the Leominster market anyway, she decided to get on and pluck them – at least she had been saved the task of slaughtering them.

Carrying them into her warm kitchen she set to work and several had been plucked when – to her consternation – she saw undeniable signs of their 'resurrection'! They were merely frozen and the warm kitchen had revived them. To her immense credit the good woman pulled herself together and made up scarlet coats for the little creatures, who must have been as shocked as she was – and even more puzzled at the situation. They wore the coats until the thaw came, added the Reverend Jobling, and nature took over. Their feathers began to grow again. It must have been fun to watch their reactions as they emerged into the open dressed in borrowed plumes, not to mention those of the other farmyard animals and birds. A real red letter day!

Adam and the Cobnash ducks may have got away with their excesses, but how did the townsfolk of Ledbury react toward the group of carousers who broke into the church on their way home and made for St Catherine's Chapel. A legend had built up that this gentle lady and much revered patron saint had left instructions that the door of her chapel must remain closed until it opened of its own accord – and then Ledbury would become the richest town in England! Unhappily that prospect flew out of the window when the drunken fellows broke open the door. Since nothing tangible was revealed the town never knew for sure how deeply it had been robbed of promised riches.

For all that Ledbury folk did not become prejudiced against cider drinking. When a calculating Chancellor of the Exchequer slapped an excise tax on cider they were not fainthearted in demonstrating against it. On the 16th July 1763 the press reported:

'A procession was made thro' the principal parts of this town by the servants of the Cyder Merchants, Coopers, Farmers, and some poor Labourers with numbers of poor people, the day the Cyder Act took place, in the following manner, viz. A man with a drum covered with black crape beating the dead march, drumsticks reverted; two mutes with crape hatbands and black cloaks; an empty barrel upon a bier carried by six poor Farmers dressed in Cyder hair cloths, with hair cloths covering the barrel, and a gauging stick in the bunghole and the pall of hair cloths supported by six others in black; two men, the one on the right with an empty can upon his head covered with crape, upon the top of which was a branch of an Apple tree, with Apples thereon, covered also with crape: the other one on the left in black, with the tools on his shoulder necessary to be made use of in felling of trees; and in the rear a number of poor objects, with apples in their bosoms covered with crape. The bells were rung muffled all the day; and every face expressed a sympathetic sorrow for the impending ruin that awaits this country.'

It must have been in these dramatic times that many brewers 'went underground' and the then Bishop of Hereford thundered at some ecclesiastical court: 'There is much secret drinking in Hereford'. He was probably right. Some verses appeared in the local press which support his contention, albeit with tongue in cheek. The lines are on display at the Hereford Cider Museum, among other fascinating material.

They read:

> 'The wild white rose is cankered
>   Along the Vale of Lugg.
> There's poison in the tankard
>   and murder in the mug.
> Along the pleasant valleys
>   where stands the white faced Kine
> Men praise the Devil's Chalice
>   And drink his bitter wine.
>
> Unspeakable carouses
>   that shame the summer sky
> Take place in little houses
>   which look towards the Wye.
> Along the Radnor border
>   And the dark hills of Wales
> Beelzebub is warder
>   And sorcery prevails.
>
> For despite Church and Chapel
>   Ungodly folk there be
> Who pluck the cider apple
>   From the cider tree
> And squeeze it in their presses
>   Until the juice runs out
> At various addresses
>   That no one knows about.
>
> And maddened by their orgies
>   Of that unholy brew
> They slit each other's gorges
>   From one a.m. till two
> Till Ledbury is a shambles
>   All in the dirt and mud;
> Where Leominster sits and gambles
>   The dice are stained with blood!'

What rejoicing there must have been in 1766 when Velters Cornewall, Herefordshire's MP, succeeded in getting the Cider Tax repealed. No wonder he was returned to Parliament in seven successive elections!

The Poet
and the
Country Maid

WE shall never know the identity of the Herefordshire
child who was playing near her mother's cottage in
Goodrich when William Wordsworth chanced along. In after
years the poet tried to trace her and failed. Perhaps it was as
well. She would have become a middle-aged woman with
Heaven knows what cares pressing upon her by 1841, for she
was not born with a silver spoon in her mouth. But at eight
years old she was enchanting, capturing the heart and imagination of the poet on this, his first visit to Goodrich Castle.

He stayed to talk with her, and the dialogue flowed so freely
that in a short time he had learned her family history. There
was nothing momentous about it. In 1793, and in her circumstances, it was probably a typical country childhood. It must
have been the artless way in which she responded to his
interest that drew from Wordsworth the warmth of feeling
which never quite faded and which inspired him to com-
memorate her in verse – 17 short stanzas repeating her story.
He called it *We are Seven*, and well into the 20th century it was
a 'party piece' at Sunday school anniversaries and family
gatherings in the English parlour.

The poet was 23 years old at the time, not an ageing man on
a sentimental journey, and on the threshold of a long career in
literature. While staying at Goodrich, accompanied by his
sister Dorothy and new-found friend Samuel Taylor Coleridge, Wordsworth took this stroll near Goodrich church and

encountered the little cottager he described in verse as having thick, curly hair, bright eyes and a light complexion. Despite her rough clothing, he confessed, 'Her beauty made me glad.' No doubt committing her description to pencil and paper within the hour ensured that her bright image was locked into his memory.

The conversation with the child opened up simply enough with the poet's kindly enquiry as to how many brothers and sisters she had:

> ' "And where are they? I pray you tell."
> She answered: "Seven are we;
> And two of us at Conway dwell,
> And two are gone to sea.
>
> "Two of us in the churchyard lie
> My sister and my brother;
> And in the churchyard cottage, I
> dwell near them with my mother." '

Pressed for further detail it transpired that after the eldest four of the family had moved away from home, the three youngest played contentedly together around the cottage and inside the churchyard, which apparently held no gloomy fears for them. Then 'Sister Jane' succumbed to some painful malady 'Till God released her of her pain and then she went away.' The brother and sister continued to play together and since their sister's grave was barely a dozen steps from the cottage door, it too formed part of their childhood games. But the little maid continued her tale:

> ' "And when the ground was white with snow,
> And I could run and slide,
> My brother John was forced to go,
> And he lies by her side."
>
> "How many are you, then," said I,
> "If they two are in heaven?"
> Quick was the little maid's reply,
> "O Master! We are seven!"

> "But they are dead; those two are dead!
> Their spirits are in heaven!"
> 'Twas throwing words away; for still
> The little Maid would have her will
> And say: "Nay, we are seven!" '

Thus the poem, rapidly drafted while Wordsworth continued his walk in the nearby grove at Alfoxden, reached its conclusion. He returned to join Dorothy and Coleridge and share his wonderment at the little girl's implicit faith and refusal to recognise any final severance in the cottager's family. He began the poem, he told them, with the last line and built the stanzas around it. When Coleridge and Wordsworth produced their joint volume of *Lyrical Ballads* a couple of years later, *We are seven* was included.

During the last 20 years of his life (he reached the age of 80), Wordsworth revisited the district four times. On each occasion he stayed at nearby Brinsop Court and brought with him his wife. On the last visit he also brought an old servant who died during their stay and went to join the little maid's brother and sister in Goodrich churchyard. By then the poet had reconciled himself to never finding the little maid again. Despite his many questions he had failed to ask the child her name.

The Case
of the
Poisoned Chocolates

WHEN Dr Thomas Hincks turned to leave Mayfield, a double-fronted, well-ordered house in Cusop Dingle, he knew he was leaving behind him a dying woman. Forty eight year old Katharine Armstrong had already lapsed into unconsciousness. 'She cannot last the day', the doctor warned her husband. It was just after nine o'clock in the morning of 22nd February 1921, and many other patients would be waiting for the doctor at his Broad Street surgery in Hay-on-Wye, a mile away. But as he was about to set out, his patient's husband begged a lift into the town so that he might reach his law practice quickly and deal with a few urgent matters.

So the two men left together on what was probably a silent drive through the charming area which housed the more successful and mainly professional families of the district. Within a very short time of the two men arriving at their respective premises, Katharine Armstrong's struggle for life ended and the nurse telephoned the solicitor's office recalling him.

Dr Hincks had no hesitation in ascribing the immediate cause of death to gastritis, though on the death certificate he added heart disease and nephritis as contributing factors to her condition. It was a certificate which was to haunt his memory for years.

At this time 47 year old Thomas Hincks had been the only GP in Hay for 23 years and was affectionately known as 'Dr

Tom'. He was a caring man with a personal concern for his patients. Mrs Armstrong had come to him less than two years before, complaining of numbness in her fingers and of muscular pain in her right shoulder and arm. The doctor diagnosed brachial neuritis and prescribed accordingly. After a few weeks the pain subsided, although a few bilious attacks occurred. It was not until August of the following year that the doctor was consulted on her behalf again, when he found clear indications of a decline, detecting a murmur of the heart and a disturbed mental condition. She was wan and listless, suffering from self reproach and delusions. This was in marked contrast to the assertive, almost self-righteous character for which she had become known to friends and guests who dined with the Armstrongs at Mayfield. So marked was the change that treatment at Barnwood, a Gloucestershire asylum, was recommended. Dr Tom rode with the solicitor and his wife on the sad journey to Barnwood.

Happily the treatment there worked well and though the authorities did not agree that the patient was ready for discharge, Mrs Armstrong's pleas to her husband succeeded and he brought her home after three months. When Dr Hincks called at Mayfield two or three days after her return home, he was relieved that his patient greeted him without rancour despite his having certified her for Barnwood. He thought her condition good, but to the doctor's disappointment, only two or three weeks elapsed before Mrs Armstrong again complained of weakness in her hands and recurring bouts of nausea. He was unable to locate the precise cause and his next visit revealed a rapid deterioration. Vomiting, abdominal pain and jaundiced skin presented the appearance of a very sick woman, and though he called at Mayfield every day thereafter he was unable to save his patient's life. A few days later the doctor's floral tribute took its place alongside the family's wreath which bore the affecting signature 'From Herbert and the Chicks'.

Five months after the Armstrongs' bereavement, Dr Hincks received a surprise – and, at first, irritating – visit from the local chemist, John Davies, who was worried about the illness of his son-in-law, Oswald Martin, a young solicitor who had settled in Hay in the closing months of the First World War and was now in charge of the firm he had joined. The chemist had the temerity to challenge the doctor's diagnosis. He doubted that his son-in-law was suffering only from a bilious attack. 'Are you sure, Doctor,' he enquired, 'that he has not been poisoned?' The doctor stifled his annoyance and asked what was on the chemist's mind. 'Oswald took tea with Major Armstrong at Mayfield yesterday,' was the reply, 'and it so happens that the Major has made several purchases of arsenic from me this year. There's something about that man. . . I don't trust him! I wonder if there's any connection – with the arsenic I mean?'

It must have seemed a preposterous suggesting involving, as it did, a highly respected local solicitor. But the chemist left the doctor looking very thoughtful. Davies then returned to his son-in-law at Bredon Hill in Cusop to communicate his suspicions. The young man's wife had had nursing training and she took her father seriously. Her husband had been violently ill on the evening of that afternoon tea party at Mayfield, though now apparently recovering slowly. But the chemist warned the young couple to be on their guard against unexpected invitations or gifts containing eatables.

Now the Martins *were* alarmed! A couple of weeks earlier they had received, through the post, an anonymous gift – a Fullers' chocolate assortment. Fortunately neither of them had a sweet tooth, but Mrs Martin had popped a few chocolates into a sweet dish while entertaining relatives. Her husband's sister-in-law, Dorothy Martin, was the only person to succumb to the temptation – and was very sick indeed throughout the night which followed. She had a high temperature and rapid pulse, but when the symptoms eased off with daylight it was assumed that Dorothy had caught a chill. And until now, no one had cause to think otherwise.

The chemist went back to his shop more worried than ever. It was market day, but at the first opportunity he checked his reference book and found it could take 15 to 20 days to completely eliminate arsenic from the body. Surely, then, he might check his suspicions by taking a sample of urine from his daughter's husband. And what about the remaining chocolates? Had his daughter disposed of them, as she had intended to do?

It so happened that she had not done so. Gingerly, she handed them over to her father. With studied care he turned over the top layer with the aid of a pencil. Two chocolates showed signs of slight disturbance and tiny particles of white powder adhered to the underside. Without more ado Davies went off to procure a well washed bottle from his shop, returned to secure a urine sample from Oswald, and set off to shatter the peace of Dr Tom's Sunday morning.

At first the doctor still could not credit the chemist's allegations and accept what was virtually a challenge to his own professionalism. But, confronted with Davies' two samples, he agreed to submit them for analysis in the strictest confidence, just four days after Oswald Martin first began to feel ill. Happily, from that day on the young solicitor began to regain strength. But the die was cast. The doctor was now in direct touch with the Home Office. The situation was so delicate that no possible hint of the inquiry must occur in Herefordshire at that stage. It might still be a terrible mistake. The waiting time was fraught with anxiety. To complicate matters even further, Oswald Martin was now being pressed by his fellow solicitor, Major Armstrong, to accept further hospitality – to tea – or to refreshments in the office over a business chat. . .

Martin stalled. It seemed incredible that a respectable older business associate who did, in fact, have legitimate legal matters to discuss, could press home invitations so openly if he had an ulterior motive. The whole inquiry might recoil upon the three 'conspirators' if Armstrong was innocent and the arsenic had been purchased, as he had assured the chemist, to make up into weedkiller. Even so, the younger solicitor knew he dared not accept the invitations. But how to stall without arousing suspicion?

So Dr Hincks pressed the Home Office for results, warning of the unbearable strain on the Martins. But when the answer came it contained no analysis – but a request that the doctor should meet the Director of Public Prosecutions together with the Chief Constable of Hereford in the latter's office at the

County Constabulary. There was no retreat now. After six long weeks of tortuous waiting, the doctor kept the appointment in Hereford and learned that the analysis confirmed the presence of arsenic in both samples submitted.

Dr Tom related the events to date and disclosed disquieting features which he had never before admitted. Though clever, well educated, self-controlled and even affable and generous at times, the Major was a womaniser and a foolish one at that. He had contracted a venereal disease which, in a churchman and do-gooder, ranked with hypocrisy. The doctor also revealed his suspicion that there lurked beneath the surface a dark side to Armstrong's nature which boded ill for anyone who crossed him.

New Scotland Yard was now called in. The detectives were puzzled about the apparent lack of motive until Oswald Martin revealed that there existed a legal problem between the two solicitors, an uncompleted property transaction which Armstrong, acting for the vendor, was unable to resolve. Pressure on Armstrong had been mounting.

So it was that on the last day of that disquieting year, Major Herbert Rowse Armstrong was astounded by the sudden, unannounced appearance in his office of the Deputy Chief Constable of Hereford with two plain clothes officers and a warrant for the solicitor's arrest. He was charged with the attempted murder of Oswald Martin. Within hours Hay-on-Wye was buzzing with astonishment at the dramatic turn of events whereby the respected lawyer with the gold-rimmed spectacles and trimly waxed moustache came to be sitting in the cells below the court in which he normally sat as Magistrates' Clerk.

In the months that followed the name of Herbert Armstrong reverberated around the whole country. Access to his home and office revealed evidence leading to an additional and more devastating charge – that of wife murder! Katharine Armstrong's body had been exhumed and found to contain arsenic. Other ominous suspicions were placed on file. Detectives and reporters besieged the little market town, heightening the sense of drama. The trial opened at Hereford Assizes on 3rd April 1922 and despite a hard fought defence by Sir

Henry Curtis Bennett, the jury reached a verdict of Guilty in less than an hour.

Exactly five months after his arrest the Major paid the supreme penalty at Gloucester Gaol, showing the same amazing composure as during his sensational trial. Would it have been a sop to his reputed vanity to know that his inscrutable expression and dapper appearance would be faithfully reproduced to become a prime attraction in Madame Tussaud's Chamber of Horrors?